OPERA ODYSSEY

Recent Titles in
Contributions to the Study of Music and Dance

Movement to Music: Musicians in the Dance Studio
Katherine Tack

The Coming of Age of American Art Music: New England's Classical Romanticists
Nicholas E. Tawa

Theological Music: Introduction to Theomusicology
Jon Michael Spencer

Philosophy and the Analysis of Music: Bridges to Musical Sound, Form, and Reference
Lawrence Ferrara

Alfred Einstein on Music: Selected Music Criticisms
Catherine Dower

Salsiology: Afro-Cuban Music and the Evolution of Salsa in New York City
Vernon W. Boggs

Dancing Till Dawn: A Century of Exhibition Ballroom Dance
Julie Malnig

Mainstream Music of Early Twentieth Century America: The Composers, Their Times, and Their Works
Nicholas E. Tawa

Televising the Performing Arts: Interviews with Merrill Brockway, Kirk Browning, and Roger Englander
Brian Rose

Johann Sebastian: A Tercentenary Celebration
Seymour L. Benstock, editor

An Outward Show: Music for Shakespeare on the London Stage, 1660–1830
Randy L. Neighbarger

The Musical Image: A Theory of Content
Laurence D. Berman

OPERA ODYSSEY

Toward a History of Opera in Nineteenth-Century America

JUNE C. OTTENBERG

Contributions to the Study of Music and Dance, Number 32

GREENWOOD PRESS
Westport, Connecticut • London

Library of Congress Cataloging-in-Publication Data

Ottenberg, June C.
Opera odyssey : toward a history of opera in nineteenth-century America / June C. Ottenberg.
p. cm.—(Contributions to the study of music and dance, ISSN 0193–9041 ; no. 32)
Includes bibliographical references and index.
ISBN 0–313–27841–5
1. Opera—United States—19th century. I. Title. II. Series.
ML1711.O88 1994
792.5′0973′09034—dc20 93–35861

British Library Cataloguing in Publication Data is available.

Library of Congress Catalog Card Number: 93–35861
ISBN: 0–313–27841–5
ISSN: 0193–9041

First published in 1994

Greenwood Press, 88 Post Road West, Westport, CT 06881
An imprint of Greenwood Publishing Group, Inc.

Printed in the United States of America

The paper used in this book complies with the Permanent Paper Standard issued by the National Information Standards Organization (Z39.48–1984).

10 9 8 7 6 5 4 3 2 1

Copyright Acknowledgment

The author and publisher are grateful to the following source for permission to reprint material:

Portions of chapter 3 originally appeared in John L. DiGaetani, ed., *Opera and the Golden West* (Madison, NJ: Fairleigh Dickinson University Press), 1993.

Contents

Preface

This study had its beginnings in 1979 as a fairly extensive article that for various reasons never reached publication. Some of the research was used in a paper read at a national meeting of the Sonneck Society for American Music, and a revised version of that appeared as an article in the International Review of the Aesthetics and Sociology of Music. When, in the late 1980s, I was asked by OperaDelaware to write an article entitled "American History Through American Opera" to accompany a Lecture/Performance series, I returned to aspects of the topic and again became fascinated by this little-known and uniquely colorful world. Subsequently I decided to attempt a history of opera in nineteenth-century America that would be aimed at the general music lover, music student, or musician. Scholars of American music are probably already familiar with much of the material, but scholars in other fields are probably not and may also find the book of interest.

I found several aspects of the project rather daunting. One was the problem of dealing with the many mixed or borderline musical works, such as melodramas or spectacles, often advertised as operas, that appeared in the first quarter of the century. Fortunately the reader could be referred to other scholars for more detailed information in this area. Another was the generally ephemeral aspect of opera performances in which other songs and musical pieces were introduced. At best opera is difficult to discuss because it has so many interlocking facets, but the added, inconsistent feature of such interpolations increases the problem. This remains, in general, unsolved, but is identified and handled as well as possible. Aside from these difficulties, sorting through, evaluating, and collating masses of information from varied sources is the lesser, if ever-present task presented by such a book.

I have not used the term "musical theater" in the title because, although it would be appropriate for the early part of the century, generally it would be misleading. Also, dates have been supplied only for people who had a telling influence on the American operatic scene.

I am grateful to many people for their help along the way. My editors, Professor Stephen Willier of Temple University's Music History Department and Eve Stone, a free-lance editor and writer, carefully and thoughtfully reviewed the manuscript and offered many helpful suggestions. Evelyn Swenson of OperaDelaware and Professor Eve Meyer, chairperson of the Music History Department at Temple University, offered the impetus to return to my lengthy but shelved project. Professor John Graziano of City University of New York and Dr. Martha Schleifer of Temple both kindly lent material. Professor Steven Kreinberg, director of graduate studies at Temple's Esther Boyer College of Music, helped with general advice and computer expertise, as did assistants in Temple's Computer Lab. Libraries that deserve thanks for their patience and aid are the New York Public Library, the Library Company of Philadelphia, the Van Pelt Library at the University of Pennsylvania, and the Library of Congress. The Inter-Library Loan staff at Temple University has efficiently and cheerfully retrieved countless works for me over the past four years. Professor John L. DiGaetani of Hofstra University's English Department has kindly given permission to reprint material that has become part of Chapter 3, which will appear in the forthcoming Opera in the Golden West, of which he is editor and which is to be published by Fairleigh Dickinson University Press. Last, the consistent support and enthusiasm of my husband and children have been of inestimable importance.

Introduction

The history of opera in the United States during the nineteenth century presents a varied, colorful panorama consisting primarily of transplanted European works. While American music scholars have produced a number of specialized studies focused on opera companies, regions, works or individuals, no survey of the subject as a whole has been undertaken for some time.[1] A few investigations have dealt, in a general way, with the development of our major musical centers, their theaters and types of repertory.[2] Although some of that repertory has been documented, some of the better-known musicians (especially star singers) studied, and the history itself divided into discrete periods, the knowledge and insights gained from scholarly work have made their way into the broader literature only slowly and sparsely. Moreover, little effort has been made to draw these strands together and weave them into a coherent narrative that tells what was performed, where, by whom, much less what the changes were and how they came about. Such is the author's purpose in this book.

The book is about musicians rather than about music, at least in the technical sense. It is based on annals, memoirs, scholarly articles and books, and some primary sources. Operas are constantly referred to, of course, and some are discussed as examples of general trends. Those examples are to some extent subjective, for with such a broad field of choices it could hardly be otherwise. As other books are readily available that recount opera plots, only those that are no longer current are outlined. Certain important personalities or troupes are given only limited mention here: for example, Henrietta Sontag, although a major figure of her time, sang opera in this country only briefly, while Alice Oates's Opera Company, which crops up in many places, has not as yet been thoroughly researched.

In the early nineteenth century, as in the final decades of the eighteenth, operas heard in the United States were mainly by English composers, thus reflecting the prominence of British culture in our society. These productions were individual in subject matter, format, language, and types of performers and so differed from other European styles.[3] Opera in America, as well as other music at that time, was in the hands of musicians of varying skill, some of whom were first-class while others were only mediocre. From 1825 to the middle of the century, operas in English reigned and then began to retreat before sporadic waves of contemporary European works, some of which then became the models emulated, with little success, by American composers. Traveling opera companies that sang either works originally in English, or French and Italian operas translated into English were later followed by Italian companies performing in that language. Both types of troupes spread the repertory of Bellini, Donizetti, and Verdi, but readers should be apprised that few familiar names will have appeared up to then. After the Civil War the compelling influence of German musical Romanticism began to have a strong effect. Telling results of this were reflected not only in an increased number of performances of German music and opera but also in the large number of American musicians who sought training in Germany. As the Wagnerian tidal wave of the 1880s receded, a more diversified repertory appeared in the 1890s. Throughout the second half of the century, opera in English remained an undercurrent.

In recent years a number of highly regarded musicologists have shifted their view from "great men and great works" to focus on music that had previously been deemed unworthy of investigation. The aim was not necessarily to search out a new masterpiece or a missed Beethoven or even lesser composer, but rather to fill in the gaps of a country's musical history and to understand the larger significance of the musicians and their works in that time and place.[4] In pursuing this point of view, musicologists emulate the efforts of thc social historians, some branches of art history, as well as some individuals in the early music movement. These groups have raised new questions, presented fresh ideas, and generally broadened the perspective of their particular disciplines. In the case of English opera, prevalent during the first quarter of the nineteenth century and intimately involved with the spoken drama, the mounting accumulation of first-class studies of American theater history has added considerably to our knowledge.[5]

The nineteenth century was a high tide of musical life in which opera thrived in both Europe and in America. As that century takes on clearer shape and substance lent by scholarly studies, a fresh look at the larger picture, the greater number of works known to us and their significance in a social context, is called for. This study, intended as an introduction, aims to review the emerging picture, offer some new perspectives, and, most important, to draw together the images of this wonderful collage of our musical culture and history.

NOTES

1. See for example, Howard Bushnell, Maria Malibran: A Biography of the Singer (University Park, PA: State University Press, 1979).

2. Julian Mates, "The First 100 years of the American Lyric Theatre," American Music I/2 (Summer 1983), pp. 22-38.

3. The eighteenth century has been covered most notably by Sonneck, Mates, Porter, and Virga. See the selected bibliography.

4. See for example, Thomas Bauman, North German Opera in the Age of Goethe (Cambridge: Cambridge University Press, 1986).

5. See for example, David Grimsted, Melodrama Unveiled: American Theater and Culture 1800-1850, (Chicago: University of Chicago Press, 1968).

OPERA ODYSSEY

1

Setting the Stage

Opera in America's past often conjures up old-fashioned, Victorian images of ample divas poised in extravagant settings. This larger than life musical genre elicits memories of a Tristan and Isolde singing their glorious love duet but too fat to embrace convincingly; an Aida richly costumed despite her slave status; foreign, legendary, half-forgotten names who reportedly sang exquisitely to create a "golden age;" and other similar associations that, by turn, may be comic, contradictory, or mysterious. In America such images emerge towards the end of the nineteenth century. As one looks back through those one hundred years it becomes evident that styles and perspectives of the picture are ever shifting. During the decades following the Civil War, European stars of celebrity status along with orchestra members, chorus and scenery journeyed across the land in lavishly equipped trains to perform in large cities and more modest towns. Throughout the 1840s and 1850s smaller, less pretentious troupes traveling much less comfortably by wagon and river sang operas in English from New York to New Orleans. In the first quarter of the century less distinction was made between opera and other theater as stock companies performed operas by English composers, plays, and other "acts" all on the same evening's bill. This is where our story starts.

Throughout the nineteenth century in this country, opera displayed a pattern that was in general analogous to that of opera in Europe in the eighteenth century. There Italian opera seria (serious opera), performed primarily by Italians in that language, had dominated courts and cities everywhere except in France. This was mainly because Italian musicians had better training, the most experience, the widest repertory, and unabashed enthusiasm for vigorously promoting themselves and their art. Similarly here as European works, at first by English and subsequently by Italian, French, and finally German composers, rose to dominate the musical scene, it was a case of experienced, well-trained performers who worked hard to advance themselves and their repertories.

Our strongest, most direct and specific cultural ties, for many years after our Revolution, were to England, so quite naturally we imported the works, music, performers, and practices of the British theater. In the first half of the 1700s London had successively seen George Frideric Handel's operas and oratorios. The former were performed by Italian singers in Italian while the latter, very similar musically to the operas, had texts and performances in English. Both helped popularize the Italian musical style Handel had learned in Italy in his youth. Meantime in the commercial theater The Beggar's Opera (premiered 1728) with its popular songs, low-life characters, spicy dialogue, and biting satire aimed at local politicians, competed keenly with Handel's sophisticated, if more staid, Italian operas. Next to their formal, glamorously aristocratic style this ballad opera, cobbled up with short popular songs, spoken parts and caustic wit, was viewed as a sort of frumpy, poor relative, unwelcome in one's parlor, if popular with the hoi polloi.[1]

After Handel's death in 1759 Italian companies virtually controlled productions at London's King's Theater, which was frequented and supported by the aristocracy.[2] Works by well-known Italian composers of the day such as Cimarosa, Piccinni, Paisiello, and others were staged there and competed with the comic operas that English composers had started to produce and which the wider public enthusiastically patronized. These English operas, following the model of The Beggar's Opera, used spoken dialogue and short songs rather than the sung recitative and florid arias of Italian opera seria. British composers were not alone in pursuing this style, for in other European countries native musicians were producing similar works. As in London, these were usually judged inferior to the Italian style operas given at court. In Vienna the idea of establishing a "national" theater took shape under Joseph II when he founded the National Singspiel, whose purpose was the promotion of home-grown German opera over Italian imports. Mozart wrote The Abduction from the Seraglio for that theater in 1782 during the same decade that he was composing his Italian-style Idomeneo, The Marriage of Figaro, and others.

American audiences at the turn of the century eagerly attended English comic operas in the Northeast, while equal fervor greeted the French opéra-comique productions staged in New Orleans, a small but strong enclave of French culture in the South. By mid-century Italian operas were gaining acceptance and after the Civil War other European works attained an exclusive, commanding position in our musical life, relegating opera in English to the hinterlands. Works by Americans were performed only in unusual circumstances and not accepted into the wider repertory. Only in the next century would American composers with a distinctive American style emerge to challenge European operatic authority.

AMERICAN BACKGROUND TO 1800: PERFORMANCES

Rather than being separate from other types of drama, comic operas were one of several items in an evening at the theater that would last three or four hours. It must have been rather like being at a variety show. The primary attractions were a main work, often a three-act spoken drama such as a play by Shakespeare or Sheridan, followed by a shorter, less serious piece, which could be a comic opera, farce, or afterpiece. Songs, dances, instrumental selections or recitations were interspersed not only between the two main works, but also between their acts to hold the audience's attention and balance the entertainment. Similar performance schemes that included different types of presentations had been customary in British and Italian theaters during the eighteenth century. Handel at times had played his own keyboard works between the acts of his Italian operas in London, and Pergolesi wrote his enduring comedy La serva padrona (The Maid as Mistress) to be staged between the acts of his "serious" opera Il prigioniero superbo (The Proud Prisoner), now relegated to the archives.

Many of the English works themselves were ephemeral in a way that seems unique to opera in general. Performances could and did vary greatly from one troupe's staging to the next, and large numbers of works remained unpublished, at least up through the first third of the nineteenth century, therefore lacking the definitive approval of the composer. Because works had to be adapted to local conditions as well as to the musical talents of the actors, revisions of text and music could take place for each new run and result in drastic alterations. Such adaptions were an accepted way of life, and if an actor, who might be responsible for forty to sixty roles or more, had not learned all of a new opera's music, he might substitute a song he already knew that would please the audience. Conversely the audience might loudly demand a favorite song, such as "Yankee Doodle," whether or not it fit the dramatic context.

Vocal scores in manuscript, consisting of the voice and bass line, possibly with some indications for instrumentation, were the usual sources for performances. It was up to one of the theater musicians to complete the harmony and copy out the instrumental parts thus created. This task probably would be undertaken by the first violinist as leader of the orchestra, or the harpsichordist who accompanied all performances. The Pennsylvania Journal notes a "band of music" (an orchestra group) in the late 1760s, and fair-sized instrumental groups were probably in use by 1770, but we may be sure that performances differed according to what instruments and players were available.[3]

GENRES

English opera, in this "British" America of the Atlantic seaboard, is a term carrying special problems of terminology that covers a wide assortment of plays with music.[4] The number and variety of productions called operas, comic operas, ballad operas, pasticcios, afterpieces, and such, all with a distinctive amount of music, form a rich if confusing diversity that reflects a spectrum ranging from the naive to the sophisticated. The first two categories are rather general, but the last three, which will be discussed first, are a bit more specific. Two elements all types held in common were spoken dialogue and the flexibility to accommodate to changing performance conditions.

Ballad operas, such as The Beggar's Opera, were primarily based on popular folk tunes with newly written words to adapt to the plot. Thus Polly's song, "O what pain it is to part" sung when she must leave her Macheath, has its newly written words set to an older Scotch folk song, "Gin thou wert mine own thing." Because the audience, of course, would know the folk tune and text, the song and its context might well take on added associations and meaning. The libretto of The Beggar's Opera dealt with questions of truth and justice, as it alluded to the immorality of prominent contemporary political figures such as Prime Minister Sir Robert Walpole and poked fun at some of the absurdities of Italian opera conventions such as the required happy ending. Macheath is miraculously reprieved at the end of The Beggar's Opera just as the "deus ex machina" would appear to set things right in the final scene of an Italian opera seria. Thus the grimness of reality is denied.

A pasticcio such as The Honest Yorkshire Man by Henry Carey, staged in New York in 1752, which opens with an "Air by Signor Porpora," attributes only a few songs to the "author," Carey. Because Nicola Porpora was an internationally famous singer and composer, his "air" was chosen as an opener. This illustrates a common eighteenth-century practice in which works of famous musicians were borrowed and used as an attraction. A composer "arranged" the opera by interspersing a few of his own pieces with that of well-known music by famous figures such as Handel, Vivaldi, Pergolesi, or others. Then the mixture was spiced up by a few judiciously placed folk tunes, and presto--a "pasticcio." Before the copyright laws, this practice was accepted and common all over Europe. Moreover, one should remember that this period, unlike what followed, was not so concerned with either artistic unity--already achieved by the international character of eighteenth-century musical style--or with a desire for strongly stamped originality, much more sought after in the Romantic age.

There were many types of "pasticcii." An example of one that contains a fair amount of music by the arranging composer is Samuel Arnold's The Castle of Andalusia, premiered in London in 1782. This typifies the English comic opera style of the period, offering familiar musical and theatrical features that look both forward and backward. It was this type of music that American audiences heard and became familiar with in theaters and at concerts. The Castle of Andalusia, which had been a great hit in London, was so well regarded that it was chosen to inaugurate Philadelphia's prestigious New Theater and was staged sporadically in other cities for a number of years.[5] The characters, including bandits and members of the wealthy Spanish nobility, reflect a "romantic" aura as does the setting of mountain caves and castles in Spain. Although this scenic ambience foretells nineteenth-century opera devices, the action does not. Rather it reflects the many inherited conventions of the eighteenth century. In Arnold's libretto, by John O'Keeffe, a series of romantic mixups and threadbare comic situations comprise the plot. Not until Act II, Scene 2, do the heroine and hero finally make contact amid a veritable maze of disguises, impersonations, and misunderstandings, comparable only to the excessive complexities of earlier Neapolitan comic opera. Emphasis is on the social divisions, wealth and pretensions of Spanish society, as well as issues of parental power and authority and filial obedience. The conflict pits youth against age's authority, ambition and ostentation. True love wins, pretension is pricked, and justice is done as the social climbing parent repents the wrongs he has done his children.

The musical score ranges, in the melting pot of the pasticcio, from folk song to Handel's "Verdi prati" borrowed from his Italian opera Alcina, and works by Arnold himself. In the opening chorus an individualistic and patriotic tone is immediately struck as we are introduced to the bandits in "Here we sons of freedom dwell, in our friendly rockhewn cell . . . valour guards our liberty." Camaraderie and a philosophy of living for the moment is rapidly established. A rousing drinking chorus is followed by a quintet that ends the act, which otherwise contains only solos. Act II, however, leans heavily on folk songs. Even "Dame nature is forming a creature so fair" by Arnold himself imitates, through its strophic setting and use of Scotch snap rhythm (sixteenth note followed by dotted eighth), a folk style. Greater complexity in "Idalian [sic] Queen to Thee we Pray," from Arnold's own oratorio, offers a contrast to the simpler songs. Act III turns to English and Italian sources, opening with Thomas Arne's lilting setting of "Hey for a lass and a bottle of cheer" in which the refrain's repetition, again, lends a folk-like cast. The ensuing Italian borrowings seem to have inspired Arnold in a similar vein, for in "The Musk Rose Blooms in Thorns and Tears" we have a longer, more elaborate and demanding aria. Musically there is something for everyone in this pasticcio, which consists of five Scotch and two Irish tunes, one piece each by Handel, Giordani, Giardini, Bertoni and Dr. Arne, with the remaining eleven pieces by Arnold himself.[6]

Musically Act I is mainly Arnold, Act II mainly traditional tunes, and Act III Italian in style. The composers Arnold drew on, Piccinni, Galuppi, Pergolesi and Scarlatti, were all well known in the late eighteenth century, their music had had broad distribution, and their popularity was reliable as an attraction. Such selections, along with the beloved English, Scotch, and Irish folk songs, and the arranger's own pieces, formed the structure of the English opera. Other "arranged" operas could reveal even more varied choices of well-known selections. The point was to create an assured "hit." If good singers were available, comic operas could be successfully staged, but how much of the original music was used and in what arrangements is difficult, if not impossible, to assess. Performances differed to a greater or lesser degree because of the reasons stated above.

Another category of English opera, the "afterpiece," was generally short, one or two acts, and gave the evening's end a good humored, optimistic feeling. William Shield's 1783 Covent Garden hit, The Poor Soldier, a favorite of George Washington, had the versatility to adapt as a main work or an afterpiece, depending on how much was cut out, or added in.[7] Perennially popular, it is a prime example of how works were altered. While the eight songs published in Philadelphia prior to 1800 reflect its popularity, the thirteen known versions of the libretto, the four known versions of the score, and other musical variables reveal the enormous flexibility common in performance.[8] The success of The Poor Soldier was due primarily to its mix of patriotism, egalitarian ideals and popular folk songs. The simple plot with a village setting was easily transposed from England to America and the hero transformed from an English soldier into a brave patriot of the Revolution of 1776. The hero, Patrick, reveals his loyalty in the following exchange with his buddy Darby:

Darby:	How did you get that beauty spot? [scar]
Patrick:	In my attempt to save the life of an officer. There I was left for dead, bleeding in my country's cause.
Darby:	Left for dead!
Patrick:	There was glory for you my boy.[9]

Through his bravery, honesty and sincerity, Patrick won the hand of the heroine and defeated the self-serving plans of her guardian, a venal and drunken priest. The familiar philosophy and traditional tunes neither taxed the mind, nor burdened the ear. Practically, the instrumental accompaniment could adapt to whatever was available no matter how simple.[10]

The libretto was by John O'Keeffe, who also wrote The Castle of Andalusia. Although popular in his day, time has not dealt kindly with O'Keeffe's plays, which now seem banal and cliché ridden. His, however, are not the worst examples of the low quality of stage works from the late eighteenth century that we inherited from England. Serious plays had generally tended to relinquish dramatic tension in favor of more sensational elements, while comedy had turned from satire, polished lines, and wit to slapstick.

The more general terms "opera" or "comic opera" were applied to many types of works, including those already discussed, but also those in which the music was written mainly by one composer. An example of the latter type is Stephen Storace's The Haunted Tower, premiered in London successfully in 1789 and first performed here in Charleston in 1793. Theater historian George Seilhamer commented:

Instead of single airs and duets to relieve the dialogue customary in English musical pieces, the story of The Haunted Tower was told in music and the success of the opera was extraordinary. Its popularity in this country was very great also, but for obvious reasons, not equal to its English reception.[11]

Storace, who studied in Naples, was probably the best trained and most talented English composer of his generation. He and his gifted sister Nancy, who created Susanna in the original production of Mozart's Marriage of Figaro, were close friends of Mozart in Vienna. Nancy was, it has been surmised, the mistress of the Austrian Emperor and later became the long-term companion of famous English tenor John Braham who eventually came to this country.[12] Storace achieved operatic success first in Vienna at the court and then in London's commercial theaters.

Storace himself composed most of the music in The Haunted Tower rather than borrowing from others, although he did use two folk tunes and appropriated pieces from some of his own operas.[13] The music in totality of conception and working-out is far closer to the Viennese Classical style of Mozart and Haydn than the simpler expression of Arnold and his contemporaries. The overture to The Haunted Tower has dramatic intensity and runs directly into the first act, thus breaking with contemporary custom that treated overtures as separate pieces not usually connected with what followed, a significant exception being Mozart's Don Giovanni of 1787. The ensembles, which are numerous and complex, advance the action rather than remaining static. Finally, because Storace wrote two of the main roles for established stars, his sister Nancy and Michael Kelly, their vocal parts are quite demanding technically. Musically this is a sophisticated and substantial work. The period, which is the time of William the Conqueror (1066), and staging, with its tower haunted by a ghost that appears in armor, foreshadow the romantic ambience of nineteenth-century opera.[14]

In sum, plays by British authors with interpolated music and songs that were staged by actors who could sing, but were not primarily vocalists, characterized English opera. These forerunners of the American musical theater, with their humorous, often satirical, topical texts, spoken dialogue, and easily remembered melodies, attracted audiences well into the nineteenth century. The music often used familiar folk songs or folk-like tunes, while accompaniments, usually consisting of strings and harpsichord, were simple. The engaging appeal of these operas remained undiminished by either their uneven quality or makeshift performances. Additions of extra musical pieces between acts, or as afterpieces to longer works, assured an evening of the desired length and variety. In a few decades specialized performers in a "star" system that drew larger audiences would eclipse the actor-singers of these stock companies. This happened first in the larger cities, but more slowly in smaller ones.

The exception to the dominance of English-style opera was New Orleans where, unlike the Northeast, the mother country was seen as France, and a substantial part of the population spoke French. In this mainly Latin-Catholic city an audience could see sporadic productions of French opera even before 1800. Little is known of these early productions, but by the turn of the century more information is available. Louisiana was not purchased from France until 1803 and not admitted as a state until 1812. By then French language opéra-comique with its unique style was comparatively well established and consistent, offering solid performances to enthusiastic audiences. This major operatic center will be discussed in the next chapter.

ASPECTS OF STAGING

Scenery, stage effects and costumes, then as now, were an important part of productions. New scenery and costumes were often advertised as an inducement to draw audiences back to a well-known drama and in some cases might help redeem the weakness of a poor play. While smaller companies relied on the sketchy suggestion of a few sets, larger more affluent ones could offer greater variety and fuller realizations.

Scenery usually consisted of a painted backcloth set in a frame and wings at the sides that provided entrances and exits for actors as well as an outline for the stage. The background of a forest, field, cottage, or tavern could be presented in this flat two-dimensional set that was then easily and quickly changed by a system of grooves through which the scenery was slid into view or out of sight. Scenery was changed in full view of the audience, as in Europe, and considered part of the "show." The curtain was opened at the beginning of a performance and closed only at the end. For practical purposes traveling troupes transported their scenery by simply rolling up the backcloths, but as the stock companies became established in city theaters by the turn of the nineteenth century, continuous travel from one town to the next was no longer necessary, and sets could be somewhat more elaborate. Later, three-dimensional additions such as bridges, rocks, and castles appeared.[15] The importance of reproducing a specific time and place was slow to develop, and thus periods were intermixed. The scene for a classical interior of Greece or Rome might be the same as that of a contemporary one. By the 1790s the New Theater in Philadelphia, which had the latest innovations in stage machinery, was employing talented professional scene painters, and stagecraft was expanding.[16]

Costumes which the actors themselves supplied often did not reflect the period as much as the affluence of the wearer. Some of the larger theaters, such as Philadelphia's New Theater, owned costumes that could be loaned to the actors, in which case wardrobe mistresses were employed to care for those collections. A few individual singers, such as Maria Garcia Malibran, sought authentic period dress early on. By the mid-nineteenth century managers and stars alike viewed costumes that reflected their time or had a glamorous quality as viable drawing cards and hence of considerable importance.

Lighting developed during the 1800s from candles or oil lamps to gas and finally electricity. In 1816 Philadelphia's New Theater changed to the use of gas light, which was more easily adjusted, and other theaters soon did likewise. Each change in the quality of lighting cast the scenery into higher relief, with its flatness more obvious and less illusory, the details of costume sharper, the colors stronger or more faded.[17] Through mid-century the custom, in European opera houses as here, was to keep the house fully lit rather than dark during the performance. This served the purpose of allowing the audience to observe who was there, greet their friends and socialize, or read the libretto if they so wished.

Needless to say this lent the theater a much more social and unrestrained atmosphere than it has today. Audiences were noisier, and actors and singers had to work hard to win their attention. Spectators expressed their disapproval, openly directing it at whoever was on stage or, if the performance had not begun, at musicians in the orchestra, a favorite target. When Mrs. Oldmixon, a well regarded and able singer, displeased her audience by her choice of a song too sophisticated for her hearers she had a fork thrown at her, and the critic noted with chagrin the audience's low level of taste.[18] Often American audiences were roundly criticized for their "lack of refinement" and rightly so if compared to audiences at European courts where order was enforced. If compared, however, to those in other theaters or opera houses, say in Naples or Palermo, American audiences were less unusual, in fact close to European patterns of behavior.

COMPANIES AND PERFORMERS

In the second half of the eighteenth century the Kean and Murray Company, the Hallam Company, and later the Old American Company, brought, from London, their repertories of farces, plays and comic operas to New York, Philadelphia, Annapolis, and other cities on the Eastern Seaboard.[19] Repeated presentations of The Beggar's Opera, Devil to Pay, Love in a Village, and The Poor Soldier attest to a consistent popularity maintained over several decades. Most actors were expected to be able to sing, but because of the nature of English opera, with its large amount of spoken dialogue, this was not a prime requisite. Talent varied and musical training was often lacking, but actors such as Mr. Wools, Miss Wainwright, and Maria Storer were singled out as possessing musical gifts and experience far beyond those of their colleagues. The first two were reputedly pupils of composer Thomas Arne, and Miss Storer was recognized as an exceptionally fine singer and actress.[20]

Stock companies were shifting by the turn of the century from a system of shared profits to one of salaried performers. Because a company staged all genres, actors were required to have enough versatility to perform in tragedy, comedy, opera or melodrama, and vocal ability was a strong advantage for actors who were hired by their ability to play a type of part such as "heavy tragedy, second comedy parts, and the first line of old women," "comic old men," "rustic, singing chambermaids" and so on, but if they could also sing they were more likely to be employed.[21]

Musical training for singers, in opera or any other medium, often rested with the composer. If he was a singer, the instruction might be comprehensive and of value. If he was not, however, his understanding of basic vocal techniques such as articulation, breath control, and tone production, would probably be limited, but he could teach the basic musical elements such as rhythm and tempo and explain the rules for ornamentation. This last, simply put, consisted of additions of notes to a melody on the part of the performer to show off technical ability and to add beauty to the piece. It was a style of singing fundamental to eighteenth-century opera that, with Rossini's works after 1815, started to wane as composers began writing out the ornamentation rather than entrusting it to the creativity of the singer.

Although Kean and Murray's first theater in Philadelphia was a warehouse near Front Street owned by Mayor William Plumstead, such makeshift stages were slowly replaced by more conventional theaters. David Douglas, the versatile manager of the Old American Company, had to arrange at least twice in his career for theaters to be built, once at "Cruger's Wharf" in New York (1758) and again there on Chapel Street (1761). Five years later hostile feelings aimed at the British, including their actors and works, erupted to destroy that theater, which was quite literally torn down by a mob.[22]

In Boston and Philadelphia antitheater sentiment emanated primarily from the clergy. Religious and moral issues were invoked in Boston with the resulting law of 1750, "An Act to Prevent Stage-Plays and other Theatrical Entertainments," a clear deterrent to opera.[23] Similarly the Philadelphia Quakers consistently opposed the stage on moral grounds and in 1759 appealed to the General Assembly to forbid construction of a theater. In conjunction the Pennsylvania Chronicle repeatedly printed articles during the late 1760s condemning the stage for its sinful and corrupting effects. Finally, the 1774 Continental Congress' antitheater law discouraged entertainment in general, and early in the following year Douglas and his company departed for Jamaica. During the Revolution musical activity was limited to performances by the military.

Although English actors incurred continuing abuse from the press, by late 1785 Hallam was presenting an expanding repertory of plays and comic operas, and within only a few years seasonal tours were being pursued that included Philadelphia, New York, Baltimore and Annapolis.[24] By 1789 an effort to circumvent the antitheater law in Philadelphia led to the advertising of "lectures" with music and "uplifting" themes. The struggle for acceptance went on for many years, and condemnation of the theater in general persisted, albeit with diminishing force, until the Civil War.

Philadelphia, seat of the federal government by the 1790s, maintained the country's most active musical life, and as skilled English managers, musicians and singers arrived on the scene, the quality of performances was considerably raised. This was a glamorous time for Philadelphia and its musical theater life. In 1794 the impressive New Theater on Chestnut Street, which combined beauty with advanced technology, opened with Arnold's The Castle of Andalusia to launch the new Wignell-Reinagle Company.[25] The troupe that graced the New Theater consisted of Miss Broadhurst (from Covent Garden), Mrs. Oldmixon, Mr. and Mrs. Marshall and the Darlys, all acclaimed actor-singers on London stages. This illustrious cast was supported by an excellent orchestra under the able direction of Alexander Reinagle (1756-1809), a first-class musician, fine keyboard performer, composer and experienced manager. From a family of musicians, he had already gained his experience and made a reputation in Edinburgh, London, and on the continent. He would exert strong leadership in the musical community in Philadelphia until his death.

The Wignell-Reinagle partnership built another theater in Baltimore, by now the third largest city in the nation, for their tours, and regular performance seasons were established there. The Old American Company, previously a serious competitor in Philadelphia, now withdrew to the more lucrative John Street Theater in New York, where singer Benjamin Carr and composer Victor Pelissier were becoming well known. Both soon moved to Philadelphia to join Alexander Reinagle and Rayner Taylor, who had previously been colleagues in London. These musicians, all of impressive caliber and accomplishment, were the focus of the city's musical life, while James Hewitt and George Gillingham added to performances and rounded out the musical scene.

This was opera in America before the turn of the nineteenth century. Yoked to other stage productions, it offered the most musical part of the evening's performance. Favorite numbers such as James Hewitt's "The Wounded Hussar," the folk song "The Blue Bell of Scotland" or "Yankee Doodle" might be requested insertions in a piece and were often delivered as performers worked to please and entertain. The audience might be unruly, but it was responsive as it rejected or approved the action on stage. Stock companies that often had family members at the core acted, sang, or danced as they moved from larger cities to smaller ones and one theater to another, secure in the knowledge that they were the only show in town.

NOTES

1. Roger Fiske, English Theatre Music in the Eighteenth Century (London: Oxford University Press, 1973), Preface.

2. Frederick C. Petty, Italian Opera in London 1760-1800 (Ann Arbor, MI: UMI Research Press, 1972), p. 30.

3. Oscar G. T. Sonneck, Early Opera in America (New York: G. Schirmer, Inc., 1915; reprinted New York, 1963), p. 24.

4. Patricia H. Virga, The American Opera to 1790 (Ann Arbor, MI: UMI Research Press, 1982), Chapter 1; Edith Borroff, "Origin of Species: Conflicting Views of American Musical Theater History," American Music II/4 (Winter 1984), pp. 101-111.

5. Fiske, English Theatre Music, p. 455.

6. Samuel Arnold, The Castle of Andalusia; score in the New York Public Library.

7. Oscar G. T. Sonneck, "The Musical Side of Our First Presidents," in Suum Cuique: Essays in Music (New York: G. Schirmer, 1916), p. 42.

8. William Shield and John O'Keeffe, The Poor Soldier, ed. William Brasmer and William Osborne (Madison, WI: A-R Editions Inc., 1978), p. x.

9. Ibid., p. 41.

10. June C. Ottenberg, "Popularity of Two Operas in Philadelphia in the 1790s," International Review of the Aesthetics and Sociology of Music XVIII/2 (1987), pp. 205-216.

11. George Seilhamer, History of the American Theater: New Foundations (1891; reprint Michigan: Scholarly Press, 1968), vol. 3, p. 108.

12. Fiske, English Theatre Music, p. 494.

13. Ottenberg, "Popularity of Two Operas."

14. Stephen Storace, The Haunted Tower (London: Muzio Clementi & Co.). Manuscript copies in Van Pelt Library at the University of Pennsylvania, Philadelphia, PA, and the Library of the Performing Arts, Lincoln Center, New York.

15. Richard Southern, Changeable Scenery: Its Origin and Development in the British Theater (London: Faber & Faber, 1952); Sybil Rosenfeld, A Short History of Scene Design in Great Britain (Totowa, NJ: Rowman and Littlefield, 1973).

16. Brooks McNamara, The American Playhouse in the Eighteenth Century (Cambridge, MA: Harvard University Press, 1969) gives ample and specific information on theaters of the time.

17. Susan Porter, With An Air Debonair: Musical Theatre in America 1785-1815 (Washington, DC: Smithsonian Institution Press, 1991). See Chapter 5 for further discussion.

18. Grimsted, Melodrama Unveiled, p. 65.

19. Sonneck, Early Opera in America, pp. 18-41.

20. Seilhamer, History of the American Theater, vol. I, p. 351.

21. Joseph N. Ireland, Records of the New York Stage 1750 to 1860 (New York: Benjamin Bloom, 1966), pp. 22, 34, 45.

22. Seilhamer, History of the American Theater, vol. I, p. 141.

23. David McKay, "Opera in Colonial Boston," American Music III/2 (1985), p. 138.

24. Seilhamer, History of the American Theater, vol. II, pp. 164-165.

25. As the company had not been ready when the theater was completed, a series of concerts had actually inaugurated it.

2

English Influence to 1825

Music, when soft voices die,
Vibrates in the memory.

Percy Bysshe Shelley

At the turn of the century Alexander Reinagle, an extremely able, versatile, and enterprising musician, was at the center of musical life in Philadelphia. This handsome man with his aquiline features and neat cravat exuded confidence and the air of the English gentleman. Born in England of a Scottish mother and Austrian musician father from whom he received his training, Reinagle gained his early musical and managerial experience in Glasgow and Edinburgh. Arriving in the New World in 1786 he arranged concerts with his colleagues in which he sang, and played the harpsichord, pianoforte, or violin. These concerts consisted of his own works, those of his contemporaries, local or European (such as Haydn and Mozart), and a sprinkling of Scotch or English folk songs. He taught keyboard instruments to members of Philadelphia's first families, including Washington's adopted daughter Nellie Custis, and supplied his students with practice material by composing and publishing collections such as his Twenty-four Short and Easy Pieces. Within these teaching materials, as in his other music, he incorporated Scottish folk songs or elements of that folk music style. Early on he sold music as well as instruments to add to his income from concerts and teaching and in 1794 extended his activities to managing the musical direction of several theaters with Thomas Wignell.[1] In that capacity he led the orchestra, from the harpsichord or piano as was then customary, wrote English style operas and arranged, often supplementing, the other musical works performed. Thus he adapted to local conditions through his many talents.

There was a continuous demand for new music because that of past composers, unlike our own day, was viewed with less interest and was somewhat limited in availability. Much of Reinagle's instrumental music was published, but the bulk of his theater music was destroyed by fires at his New Theater on Chestnut Street. Considering the superior quality of his remaining works, this is a great loss.

The use of familiar folk tunes in concerts touched a nostalgic chord in many, evocative of their homeland and past. Folk songs had recently crested in popularity in the British Isles, causing numerous collections and settings to be published, so Reinagle's various use of these tunes, as he blended them with his classical style, was similar to practices of his contemporaries.[2] Such links and adaptions, musical and psychological, were common to many of the new immigrants for whom establishing a shared sense of national unity meant, in part, resolving the conflicts and complexity surrounding the question of British and American identity. Although the Revolution as well as the War of 1812 had pockets or even sizeable areas of English sympathizers, an overriding American patriotism would eventually prevail to unify diverse groups.

THE BACKDROP

As the new nationalism gathered momentum it found one focus in the admiration for the heroes of the Revolution and political leaders who followed and another in ideas and planning for incipient institutions. While President Washington remained most revered as the "Father of His Country," a special aura also surrounded other celebrated patriots and their initiatives. One such was Stephen Decatur's dramatic recapturing of the U.S. frigate Philadelphia in 1804 in the war against Tripoli. We had become embroiled in this conflict in 1801 because we refused to increase the tribute demanded by the Barbary pirates of Algiers, Tunis, Morocco, and Tripoli in exchange for trade. The colorful, intense drama of that distant war and its courageous seamen became grist for novels, plays, and operas as Mediterranean pirates, sea battles, and naval heroes crowded into print and onstage, attracting enthusiastic readers and audiences. One example was Samuel Arnold's opera *The Veteran Tar*, first staged in London in 1801, that was rewritten to reflect an American view of the war and times. Thus transformed, it became *The Tripolitan Prize* in New York (1802) and later *American Tars Triumphant* in Boston. In Philadelphia Reinagle added music to the British pasticcio *The Naval Pillar* which would appear six years later as *Tars from Tripoli* with the subtitle *A Tribute of Respect to the Mediterranean Heroes*.[3] With our victory over Tripoli the most exciting and absorbing news of the day, these depictions of battles of brave sailors against evil pirates successfully drew audiences to give expression to powerful nationalistic feelings. Such patriotic themes were repeated in the many varied settings of Thomas Morton's play *Columbus; or a World Discovered* and frequently appeared in other theatrical genres. Again embattled in the War of 1812, we successfully asserted ourselves and won against a strong outside enemy. Our self confidence and sense of national pride was strengthened despite the war's lack of popular support and the economic hardship of the British blockade on the eastern seaboard.

The individual soldier of the Revolution was also idealized. We find him in the character of Patrick in *The Poor Soldier*, the favored comic opera, whose durable quality kept it on the stage until the 1840s. The play mercilessly satirizes its one French character, Bagatelle, and casts unflattering aspersions on the heroine's guardian, a Catholic priest. A largely Protestant population, undisturbed by such blatant national or religious prejudice, accepted these derogatory portrayals without a qualm. Protestant preachers in fact frequently denounced Catholicism and its evil agent the Pope as an imminent menace against which one must constantly guard.

Any theater, no matter how patriotic its productions, came under the fire of religious groups who were outspoken in their condemnation of the stage as a swamp of sin that could tempt even the most devout. The established clergy of New England, Philadelphia Quakers, Presbyterians of Virginia, Episcopalians, as well as the westward moving Baptists and Methodists, all agreed on this point: the evils of the theater. They declared their views in sermons and pamphlets with supporting references from prestigious contemporaries and even drew on accepted icons such as Plato, Aristotle, Rousseau and others for arguments. Ministers compared the theater "pit," now known as the orchestra, to the "pit" of hell and attacked profanity on stage as well as stage references to God (positive or negative), the costumes, the actors themselves, and the audience. This censure was not entirely without provocation. One should remember that until well into the nineteenth century many American theaters, like their British counterparts, designated a particular section for prostitutes, thereby making them available and an accepted part of the audience. In addition, space was routinely leased in theaters for bars to sell liquor to patrons. The prostitutes, who were sometimes given free tickets, were supposed to attract a larger audience (and probably did), while the bars helped support the theater financially. Moreover, the overriding message of the drama could well be that described by Presbyterian minister Samuel Miller as one in which "piety and virtue are made to appear contemptible, and vice, in the person of some favorite hero, is exhibited as attractive, honorable, and triumphant."[4] Significantly the Bible was the most popular of books in America at this time, and the aim of the American Bible Society founded in 1816 was to place a Bible in every home.

The establishment of institutions signified a wish to preserve our history and recognize and develop our visual arts and music. The Pennsylvania Art Academy, which shocked our rather staid citizens with a reproduction of the nude Venus de Medici in 1805, was prominent among these. New York's American Academy of Fine Arts, the American Antiquarian Society at Worcester, and the Handel and Haydn Society of Boston were all founded within the next ten years. Despite these important emblems of civilization, the Evening Post of 1818 offered a pithy view of city life and its daily problems as it repeatedly complained about the number of pigs allowed to roam uncontrolled in the streets of New York.

Philadelphia managed to hold its position of eminence in the theatrical sphere of the North until the 1820s, even though it lost its position as capital of the country and even of Pennsylvania in the 1790s. The city saw, until 1830, close to 220 out of 258 works performed in English, of which 155 were from the three major London theaters.[5] These works included music to varying degrees. Strong British ties extending throughout the cities of the Atlantic seaboard linked all aspects of music and theater and would remain unbroken until the 1840s. Acknowledgment of those British roots is evident in the nickname of "Old Drury," borrowed from London's famous theater, not only for Philadelphia's much admired New Theater, but also for theaters in New York, Boston, and elsewhere.

That other operatic pole of the country, New Orleans, enthusiastically supported opéra-comique from Paris. This functioned not only as entertainment but also as a strong cultural link to the homeland. In the first quarter of the century and up to the Civil War, New Orleans, with its Parisian repertory, singers, and dancers, remained an innovative and lively operatic center.

REPERTORY, COMPOSERS, MUSIC

English composers dominated the theater in the North. Musicians, such as Alexander Reinagle, Rayner Taylor, James Hewitt or Benjamin Carr, came from London to spread their knowledge and repertory through teaching and concerts, thus providing models of training and style. German Gottlieb Graupner in Boston and French Victor Pelissier in New York and Philadelphia composed, arranged, and rearranged music for the theaters. The music came mainly from London and the musicians adapted their style to it, using the imported comic operas as models for their own work. Folk tunes, particularly from England, Scotland, and Ireland, were frequently included.

In sharp contrast to today's practice, operas in the early nineteenth century were identified by the librettist with little or no mention of the composer. Here we will identify works by composer, but the reader should be aware that the music may have been "arranged" by several different hands and at various times. Usually the texts of the operas needed to be shifted to an appropriate American locale and their characters Americanized or modified so that the whole would have greater relevance and audience appeal. Ballad operas, pasticcios, melodramas, and spoken dramas, all interspersed with songs, dances, recitations, and other theatrical acts shared the same stages and the same evening's bill in true egalitarian fashion.

An important group of works to achieve popularity here were the successful hits in London by English composers who never came to these shores. A few of these transplanted pieces that had endured from the latter part of the eighteenth century would include The Children in the Wood and The Agreeable Surprise by Samuel Arnold; Lock and Key, The Poor Soldier, and The Highland Reel by William Shield; No Song, No Supper and The Prize by Stephen Storace; and The Padlock by Charles Dibdin. By the second decade of the nineteenth century, Henry Bishop's many operas had a continuous vogue, and in the early 1820s Clari, the Maid of Milan, with libretto by American writer-actor John Howard Payne, became his most famous work. Clari, with only six musical pieces, included the song "Home, Sweet Home," which Bishop used as a recurring musical theme. This long-lasting hit would come close to the status of a national anthem in years to come. Given the popularity of Clari, which emphasizes filial love, morality, and acceptance of one's true station in life, one can understand more clearly the appeal of "Home, Sweet Home." The flavor of the text is revealing and bears repeating:

'Mid pleasures and Palaces though we may
  roam,
Be it ever so humble there's no place like
  home!
A charm from the skies seems to hallow us
  there,
Which seek through the world, is ne'er met with
  elsewhere.
  Home! Home, sweet sweet Home!
There's no place like Home! There's no place like Home!

An Exile from Home, Splendour dazzles in
vain!
Oh! give me my lowly thatch'd Cottage
again!
The Birds singing gaily that came at my
call,
Give me them with the peace of mind dearer
than all!
Home! Home, sweet sweet Home! etc.[6]

The song appears at a crucial moment and expresses one strong aspect of the heroine's current dilemma, which concerns the lure of her high born lover and the temptations of luxury, as opposed to her morality and obligation to return to her parents and humble home.[7] We may assume from the subsequent popularity of the song that this combination of seduction, reconciliation, and penance of some sort touched a truly resonant chord in many.

Among the other works noted, Stephen Storace's popular comic opera No Song, No Supper, premiered in London in 1790, appeared here frequently from 1792 until 1847. Like Shield's The Poor Soldier it could serve as the main attraction, for it lasts approximately an hour and a quarter, or shrink to afterpiece length, but there any resemblance ends, for Storace's graceful, charming music is far better constructed. Its slight, comic libretto concerns the trials of two couples whose intent to marry has been thwarted by their families. The parents ambitiously plan for their daughters to marry into wealthy families and so view the chosen suitors as poor prospects. The couples, after several broad, comic episodes involving minor characters, and in one sequence a venal lawyer, are then fortuitously reunited. Humorous situations, the virtue of the main characters, and the triumph of good over greed gave the libretto its moralistic if simplistically stated appeal, and the music added to its attraction.

Storace composed new music for about half of No Song, borrowed some from his own past works and about a third from music by other composers. Doubtless these borrowings were advertised as an attraction for the audience. The composer took two songs from operas by his French contemporary, André Grétry, one of which ("Oui, noir, mais pas si diable," "Yes, black, but not like a devil") had become very popular (with new words) during the French Revolution. While Storace borrowed the second part of the Act I Finale from his own Italian opera La cameriera astuta (The Clever Chambermaid), most of the other songs were newly composed, short and strophic (that is, with several verses set to the same tune).[8] There were ensembles for the principal singers, but no chorus. As already noted, at best only sketchy piano-vocal scores made their way to this country, and so chords had to be filled in and orchestration written out by one of the company's resident musicians.

Unfortunately, this first class composer died in his early thirties, leaving more fragments than complete works. During his stay in Vienna, he had composed two successful operas given before the emperor, one of which was a collaboration with Mozart's famous librettist Lorenzo da Ponte, who wrote the texts for Don Giovanni, The Marriage of Figaro and Così fan tutte (All Women Do Thus). We will meet the versatile and gifted da Ponte again in New York.

English translations of foreign works occasionally appeared to amplify the repertory. One of the best known in the early 1820s, and for long after, was Carl Maria von Weber's Der Freischütz (The Freeshooter). This innovative work mapped out the terrain for German Romantic Opera for the next thirty years. Premiered in Berlin in 1821 to enthusiastic audiences, three years later it was playing in London in seven different English adaptions.[9] The core of Weber's idea for this piece was to create an integrated musical-dramatic entity and in so doing he reflected a number of the strains of German Romanticism. He chose a libretto based in part on a folk tale, used a few references to folk tunes and, following the style of the old German singspiel (sung play), used spoken dialogue. These elements, combined with its distinctive features, united to give the whole its nationalistic flavor. The drama focuses on a love story in which the hero, Max, must win a contest of marksmanship to marry his beloved Agathe. To ensure success he makes a pact with the devil, who promises to guarantee the bullets' accuracy through his magic. In return the evil one will receive the usual--Max's soul. The pact is made and the bullets cast in the eerie "Wolf's Glen" scene set at midnight, where Max and his friend Caspar, who is already in thrall to Samiel (the devil), meet. This scene, which gave the opera much of its attraction, became a model of the supernatural horror scene for subsequent composers. This melodrama, as the scene was called, has exciting action with musical accompaniment and spoken dialogue that alternates with dialogue over music. The idea had come from earlier French composers to become a well-used theatrical and operatic device. An earlier example is the grave digging scene in Act II of Beethoven's Fidelio (premiered in 1805). In the Wolf's Glen scene, wonderfully colorful orchestration and unusual harmonic modulations added to the atmosphere of ghostly shadows, low thunder, ominous, flapping owls, and other suggested horrors as Caspar invoked the evil one and bargained with him. Weber contrasted the healthy outdoor life of the German forester (Max) with the powers of darkness that culminate in the shooting match that symbolically pits good against evil.

The continuous music, with fewer pauses for arias, imaginative orchestral color, and some use of recurring motifs combined distinctively to offer a type of opera that departed from the usual classical models. Furthermore the spoken dialogue lent the familiar sound and format of the English operas. While Weber's complex work appeared in watered-down or distorted arrangements made for the London or American stage, even those versions had great popularity. By the late 1820s in this country Freischütz was promoted by English singer-composer Charles Edward Horn who, as a major figure in our theaters for twenty years, excelled in the role of the villainous Caspar.

Another category of popular operas was by musicians who immigrated here and settled to stay. A brief list of the more prominent works would include Alexander Reinagle's Columbus, or A World Discovered and The Volunteers; James Hewitt's Tammany, or The Indian Chief; Benjamin Carr's The Archers, or The Mountaineers of Switzerland and Bourville Castle; Victor Pelissier's Edwina and Angelina and The Wife with Two Husbands; Rayner Taylor's Buxom Joan, Capocchio and Dorina, and The AEthiop; or, Child of the Desert; and John Bray's The Indian Princess. Destructive theater fires, which were dealt with by volunteer firemen using rather primitive equipment, were frequent in the eighteenth and nineteenth centuries, and consequently much of the music of those days has been lost. Fortunately the last two works survived and have been restored in modern editions.

Rayner Taylor was a well trained, successful London composer whose career, like Reinagle's, could serve as a prototype of the versatile, immigrant musician of the time. Having left London in his late forties (apparently with a younger female student) to settle at Philadelphia in 1793, this energetic, gifted man was a music teacher, copyist, singer, music seller, organist at St. Peter's church, and composer. In London he had been Reinagle's teacher, and the two met again in Philadelphia to collaborate on several musical works. In the case of Pizarro, or The Spaniards in Peru (based on Kotzebue's drama), the music is unfortunately lost. A score, however, of Taylor's The AEthiop: or, The Child of the Desert, survives and the first performance took place in Philadelphia on New Year's Day, 1814. An earlier musical setting, by Henry Bishop, had failed in London even with some revisions and enhanced by the glamour of the famous star Charles Kemble. Taylor's version, on the other hand, was popular for several decades. The main plot centers on Harun al-Rashid's concern for a potential rebellion, while the comic subplot deals with a young Greek husband and wife who are liquor dealers defying prohibition in Baghdad. Some of its choruses are reminiscent of Handel's, whose works Taylor had known in London, while certain of the "airs," vocal ensembles, and instrumental pieces clearly reflect the style of Mozart or Haydn. The high quality of Taylor's music with its engaging charm and lilt doubtless played a large part in the lasting success of the work.[10]

THE SOUTH: NEW ORLEANS

Meanwhile at the southern end of the settled country in New Orleans, another type of opera prevailed: French opéra-comique. The season of 1805-1806 saw the beginnings of consistent performances and included approximately sixteen works by a cluster of contemporary, successful composers in Paris, among them the above-mentioned Grétry, Nicolas Dalayrac, and Francois-Adrien Boieldieu. Grétry's Richard Coeur-de-Lion (Richard the Lionheart), premiered in Paris in 1784 where it is periodically revived to this day, was acclaimed in New Orleans as well as the French capital. Many of the other popular operas persisted in the repertory from ten to twenty years but lacked the quality or universal appeal needed for a longer life. Undoubtedly the quality of performances varied considerably, as in English opera, because the standard practice of cuts and changes had to be followed to accommodate the abilities of the singers. One may speculate, however, that performance quality rose when in November 1819 a new company and "band" (as theater orchestras were called), some of whom had been imported from France, opened the Orleans Theater with François-Adrien Boieldieu's two-act Jean de Paris (John of Paris), first staged in Paris in 1812, and Henri Berton's one-act Les Maris garçons (Boys as Husbands), premiered in 1806. Both Boieldieu and Berton were prominent composers in Paris, the former famous for his many masterly operas and the latter of equal fame, if lesser talent. The performance was preceded by an instrumental piece, "March of General Washington."[11]

Works in this repertory of opéra-comique, some of which predated the French Revolution, consisted of from one to three acts, covered a wide range of subjects, some more serious than comic, and were characterized by their use of spoken dialogue. Choruses, if not cut in performances, probably were sung by only a few singers, and in like manner the instrumental entr'actes were viewed as optional and may have been replaced by other selections. As part of the entertainment the use of an afterpiece was also common.

Although French and English operas clearly had certain elements in common, the music in the former was usually of a much more sophisticated quality, more often identified with one composer, and seemed to depend less heavily on "borrowing" and the use of folk tunes. Significantly, French opera composers had a long, solid musical tradition of both serious and comic works that supported and nurtured their development. Dances, instrumental interludes, fairly short songs, and dialogue shaded the textures of

French opera. English composers, on the other hand, came out of a theater history more oriented to the spoken drama in which music's role was subordinate and acting took precedence over singing. An important difference between the two genres is that if the sung sections of the French comic opera are removed, the remaining spoken play often fails to make sense, and this is not as consistently the case with the English opera. Although the French plots reflect some universally popular themes shared with the English, each type of libretto clearly reveals the roots and culture from which it emerged in terms of language, references, and musical style.

The repertory in New Orleans included operas of either well-known eighteenth-century French composers or popular contemporaries. By 1806 the energetic manager Louis Tabary, who gave the city strong theatrical leadership, had become director of the St. Peter Street Theater. Not content with one theater, he opened a second, the Théâtre de la Rue St. Philippe, two years later with a production of Étienne-Nicolas Méhul's one-act opera Une Folie (A Folly), which had premiered in Paris in 1802. In New Orleans, a city of about 15,000, two theaters staged operas on alternating nights with ballets interspersed and occasional time out for drama or other entertainment. The intensity is astonishing. From 1806 to 1810 the New Orleans audiences witnessed over three hundred performances of more than seventy different operas.[12] Especially popular were works by Grétry and his disciple, Nicolas Dalayrac. All classes, including African-Americans (free and slaves), were welcome at the theater, because all social groups were considered necessary to sustain theatrical economy and survival.[13]

Grétry's Richard Coeur-de-Lion, reported to be a favorite of John Adams, was based on the romanticized tale of Richard the Lion-Hearted, son of the French Eleanor of Acquitaine, his imprisonment following a Crusade, and his subsequent rescue by the faithful minstrel Blondel.[14] First produced in Paris in 1784, Grétry's imaginative and forward-looking opera rivaled the popularity of Beaumarchais' concurrently running play Le Mariage de Figaro, later made immortal by Mozart. Music and libretto, by poet Michel-Jean Sedaine, combined in an arresting work in which the setting of the remote past, here the Gothic period, anticipated a vogue that would be strongly favored by nineteenth-century composers and librettists.[15] Likewise, Grétry's use of a recurring musical theme, although novel in opera at the time (it preceded Freischütz and Clari by almost forty years), would become an important technique in the nineteenth century and reach its ultimate expansion in the works of Wagner. Richard's imprisonment in a castle gave ample opportunity for dramatic visual effects. The gloomy, oppressive castle of Linz in Act I, with its heavy walls and towers, emphasizes the grimness of Richard's imprisonment. When master and minstrel finally meet, the king is on a terrace, isolated but within the castle and enclosed by iron gates, while Blondel is below. The meeting occurs as dawn is breaking, but through the music rather than visual contact. Richard and Blondel, who is disguised as an old, blind street fiddler, are separated and hidden from each other. Blondel plays the rather simple tune well known to Richard and from there their "recognition" unfolds. This scene in Act II is the high point of the opera, and from then on the action revolves around freeing Richard. Incidentally, Richard's betrothed has also arrived at the castle so that in due course we can have the appropriate happy ending. The combination of these kinds of dramatic visual effects to heighten the suspense, the emphasis on personal loyalty, and the novel use of the recurring musical theme, was exciting, unusual, and captivating.[16] This "rescue" theme in opera had been popular in France in the 1780s and 1790s, but the most famous example, Beethoven's Fidelio, was composed after the turn of the century.

From 1812 to 1815 the war cast a pall over theaters in general (those that it did not close outright), but at its end a crucial figure for New Orleans and French opera appeared: manager John Davis. He undertook the rebuilding of the recently burned Orleans theater, imported actors and musicians from Paris, and was noted in his obituary as the man "who gave Louisiana a French Theatre."[17] Born in Paris in 1773, Davis arrived in New Orleans when he was thirty-six to enter a variety of business enterprises that finally included the Orleans Theater. This opened in November 1819, as noted, with the two tried-and-true operas by Boieldieu and Berton, Jean de Paris and Les Maris garçons, some new imported members of the company, and veteran Louis Tabary as manager. Davis undertook a trip to France in the spring of 1822 to hire new musicians, singers, and a professional ballet. He also acquired the French version of Rossini's Barber of Seville. By this time, however, a new type of competition had appeared in New Orleans in the form of an English opera company.

James Caldwell, originally recruited in England as a leading actor for the "Charleston Company of Comedians," had brought English operas to New Orleans with his Virginia Company. Although at least one other English company had preceded him, he was the first to establish a permanent English theater there, namely the American Theater in Camp Street, which opened in January of 1824. Caldwell had made his American debut in 1816 in Charleston and undertook the dual role of actor-manager a year later in Washington. He built a theater in Petersburg, Virginia, played on the southern circuits of Alexandria, Norfolk, Richmond, and Fredericksburg, and arrived in New Orleans with his Virginia Company at the St. Philip Theater in 1820. A month later they moved to the Orleans Theater, which they shared on alternate nights with Davis's French company. The initial repertory included Henry Bishop's Guy Mannering (based on the Scott novel), Charles Horn's London hit The Devil's Bridge with the fine Irish tenor Arthur Keene, Samuel Arnold's The Children in the Wood, Arne's Love in a Village, and other favorites. Following his first two-month season, Caldwell would return for three consecutive years to the Orleans Theater and eventually would build his own theater, patterned on the famous Chestnut Street Theater in Philadelphia.[18]

By 1823 the company included Jane Placide, an attractive, versatile actress-singer from a large family of well known actors, who rapidly became a local celebrity and performed on the New Orleans stage for many years. She sang in the English version of Boieldieu's popular Jean de Paris many times, as it became a staple in the English opera repertory and also appeared in The Devil's Bridge with the reputable actor-singer Thomas Phillips. He had accumulated accolades in New York a few years previously and had been praised in Philadelphia as a fine singer who was the first to use the Italian method.[19] His tour of the country eventually took him to New Orleans where he appeared in The Barber of

Seville, probably in Bishop's adaption.

As the English-speaking population increased, French opera became, especially in hard economic times, a patriotic rallying point used by those calling for the support of French culture and hence French music. Both English and French opera articulated the two heritages of New Orleans, also making it a major operatic center of the new country.

OTHER SOUTHERN CITIES

Two other important Southern centers, both under the influence of English opera rather than French, were Charleston and Richmond. At the Charleston Theater by 1800, Alexander Placide, formerly "first Rope Dancer to the King of France and His Troop" and subsequently father of a large family of actors, among them Jane of New Orleans fame, was manager.[20] The Placides well illustrate the fact that acting was often a family undertaking and business. Under the wing of a husband and in the setting of a family, an unmarried daughter or a respectable married woman, despite the inevitable notoriety associated with actresses, could earn her living in the theater with little criticism. Children were often pressed into service early, on stage or off, in this financially unstable occupation. An early apprenticeship within the family enterprise could produce some fine actors, as in the case of the Placides.

Alexander Placide divided his company's winter and spring seasons of English plays and comic operas between Charleston and Savannah. Fashionable Charleston had an elegant society patterned on the English tradition with a clear class structure that even included a famous Race Week in February. To this audience Placide brought plays, comic operas, novelties and famous stars. He remained as manager of the Charleston Theater, although until his death in 1812 he expanded his scope to include theaters in other cities. Charleston was the city that attracted James Caldwell in 1816 as a leading actor for the "Charleston Company of Comedians," and in the following year musician Charles Gilfert became manager and leader of the orchestra and would remain there until 1825. Storace's No Song, No Supper and The Haunted Tower, Samuel Arnold's dependable favorites, The Agreeable Surprise and The Children in The Wood, along with many others, accompanied the Shakespearean fare and popular plays by Sheridan, making it possible to offer several productions a week during the particular months that made up the "seasons."[21]

Richmond had an equally busy and varied theatrical life in which the enterprising Placide had become involved early on as an actor and then in 1809 as a manager. On the night after Christmas in 1811, when Thomas Attwood's comic opera The Adopted Child was to be performed, the Richmond theater burned, killing a large part of the full-house audience. As the disastrous loss of life became known, outpourings of condolences and sorrow came from other sections of the country, and Congress even passed a resolution for a month of mourning. The fire had a particularly numbing effect on audiences, for people were afraid to gather in public places in large numbers for some time to come. The clergy, predictably, declared that this was a sign of divine anger and punishment, and in fact a church was eventually built on the theater's site. A devastating musical effect was that all of the musical scores, parts, and playbooks went up in the terrible conflagration.[22] Finally a new theater was built in 1819, which lasted until the Civil War. It was opened by Gilfert, who had been touring with the Charleston company and recently played in Norfolk. One of the actors was John Bray, and an advertisement for The AEthiop listed the music as by Gilfert, but this probably meant he "arranged" Taylor's music. Gilfert would later become manager at the Bowery Theater in New York.

In both the South and New England troupes traversed a number of theatrical circuits that had been in existence for some time, using a larger town as a base.[23] The number and types of works staged, from operas to dramas, were often impressive, especially as the repertory of the company had to be limited by the number and capabilities of the players.

Southern circuits were linked by theaters in the larger coastal cities already noted and also in smaller ones such as Fredericksburg and Petersburg. One rather extensive route that included Charleston, Savannah, Columbus, and New Orleans took fifty to seventy days to cover each way.[24] Another less ambitious one was that of Columbus, Tuskegee, and Auburn. Enterprising managers Sol Smith, Noah Ludlow, and James Caldwell, with their players and mixed repertory, crossed and recrossed these circuits accompanied by wagons transporting scenery and costumes. If the company orchestra was too small or a minor role needed to be filled, local amateurs were temporarily recruited, thus adding a more personal touch to the performance. If there were skilled singers in the company, more musicals could be performed; otherwise dramas and melodramas were emphasized. Playbills to advertise the entertainments were posted and handed out by the actors themselves. The theater in Savannah was attractive enough to draw London-trained musician James Hewitt and his son John in the early 1820s. James left in 1823 when the theater burned, but John remained to open a School of Music in Augusta for a brief period and noted the many Italian and German music teachers in Southern small towns.[25]

THE NORTHEAST: PHILADELPHIA AND NEW YORK

As in the South, Philadelphia and New York troupes resorted to touring when audiences waned. The team of Alexander Reinagle, as musical manager, and Thomas Wignell, as theater manager, had ensured consistency for their Philadelphia company's tours by building theaters in Baltimore and Washington. Theirs was a strong stock company, highly organized by Wignell with clear regulations as to the requirements of rehearsals, performances, sobriety, and other areas in which problems frequently arose. Wignell's death in 1803 coincided with the growth of the "star" system that eventually would undermine the stock companies. Reinagle devoted most of his energy to the musical direction of the large and varied repertory of the theaters where, as Durang described,

> He presided at his pianoforte looking the very personification of the patriarch of music--investing . . . [it] with a moral influence reflecting and adorning its salutary uses with high respectability and polished

manners. His appearance was of the reverend and impressive kind, which at once inspired the universal respect of the audience. Such was Reinagle's imposing appearance that it awed the disorderly of the galleries. . . . No vulgar, noisy emanations were heard from the pit of that day.[26]

At Reinagle's death in 1809, preceded by that of one of the company's mainstays, notable actress Mrs. Merry, the company was turned over to co-managers William Warren and William Wood. This team usually kept about forty actors in the company. In the 1810-1811 season they staged fifty-five plays, about a quarter of them by Shakespeare, and fifty-four afterpieces. According to a letter in the Mirror of Taste (November 27, 1809), the audience was as noisy and obnoxious as the actors were proper and the plays moral. The liquor available in the unheated theaters in winter months doubtless helped to warm the audience, but at the same time it weakened inhibitions.

From about 1816 the Philadelphia circuit (including Baltimore and some summer seasons in Washington) showed a decline in profits, in part because of an economic depression that caused banks and businesses to fail. The crisis lasted until 1822, and in addition the theater circuit saw two terrible fires in 1820. One destroyed the New Theater in Philadelphia on April 2, the other demolished the Washington theater two weeks later on April 18. Of the Philadelphia theater fire, actor-manager William Wood noted in his Personal Recollections that "The library and music were of an extent and value unknown to any other American theatre."[27] With remarkable resilience, the two managers erected a new theater on the same spot in 1822 and called it, of course, "Old Drury." Nonetheless, declining profits and growing competition, coupled with the financial burdens of the star system and losses of music, scenery, costumes and numerous other necessities from the disastrous fires, took a heavy toll, and in 1825 Warren and Wood dissolved their partnership. Crowning blows came to Philadelphia's prime theatrical position in the late 1820s when the rivalry among the Chestnut Street, the Arch Street, and the Walnut Street Theaters resulted in economic disaster and several companies rapidly failed. During this decade Philadelphia and New York had gradually shifted places in the theater world as New York's wealth increased, and its strategic position as a port of entry for players and their theatrical endeavors became crucial.

Composers with the greatest number of comic operas performed in Philadelphia this first quarter century included Arnold, Kelly and Bishop. Besides The Castle of Andalusia discussed earlier, Samuel Arnold composed music for The Maid of the Mill (based on Richardson's widely read novel Pamela), The Agreeable Surprise, and many others. Michael Kelly had about eighteen pieces staged, including Blue Beard and The Forty Thieves. It is reported in his Memories that he only wrote the melodies for his operas, which indicates that harmonization and instrumentation would have been done by others.[28] This famous tenor had created the roles of Basilio and Curzio in Mozart's Marriage of Figaro and was a close friend of the Storaces. Henry Bishop, first known through his "arrangements" of works of Mozart and Rossini, produced the popular Clari, the Maid of Milan in 1823.

In New York William Dunlap was manager of the Park Theater at the turn of the century with the popular actor-singer John Hodgkinson and his family as the core of the troupe. By 1805 Dunlap had retired bankrupt from the theater and Hodgkinson, his wife, and sister-in-law were dead, leaving the two orphaned Hodgkinson children. For the next few years in New York many of the identifiable musical works appear more consistently as afterpieces than as the central attraction, whereas in Philadelphia Reinagle programmed and encouraged lengthier musical pieces, despite the inevitable extra expense they incurred.

The expense was worth it in the case of The Indian Princess, first staged at Philadelphia's New Theatre in 1808 and a year later in New York as a benefit. Its choice as a benefit implied as a matter of course that it had a following and expectations of financial success. The Indian Princess, a collaboration between American writer James Nelson Barker and English actor-musician John Bray, is a milestone among American works because of the subject matter and because a complete score was published, an unusual undertaking for that time. Individual songs were often published but rarely a complete score. The title page of The Indian

Princess describes it as "An operatic melo-drame. In three acts" which meant that besides the songs, vocal ensembles, and instrumental pieces, illustrative background music was added to some of the action to intensify particular dramatic moments. Although not the first play on an Indian subject, The Indian Princess is probably the first on the tale of Pocahontas and Captain John Smith. Indian subjects would attain great popularity as we know from John Stone's highly successful play, Metamore, which won the first drama prize given in this country in 1829. It was offered by actor Edwin Forrest, who then made the play famous by making the title role one of his acclaimed specialties.

While the songs and ensembles of The Indian Princess are quite simple, some, such as "When the Midnight of Absence," have a certain grace and charm. A humorous, nonsensical turn appears in "Och! Hubbaboo! Gramachree! Hone!" set to music with a folk-like lilt. The instrumental inserts to accompany action, as when the "Indians assemble & prepare for war," are the reason for Bray's use of the term "melo-drame." Interestingly enough, unlike the English comic opera, little of the music is optional and in fact has to be retained if the work is to make sense.[29]

There was now a steadier stream of comic operas produced in New York, flowing mainly from the Park Theater. Arnold's Castle of Andalusia and Maid of the Mill, Arne's Love in a Village, Storace's Siege of Belgrade, Horn's Devil's Bridge, and others became the heart of a repertory to be played and replayed. They were performed often by first class singers such as English tenor Charles Incledon, whose beautiful voice had been greatly admired in London and who was later described as "probably the best singer who had ever appeared in Philadelphia."[30]

One of the most popular operas, The Devil's Bridge, a collaboration between Charles Edward Horn and English tenor John Braham of European fame, was first performed in London in 1812, arrived in New York in 1815 and was still on the stage in the 1840s. The play by Samuel J. Arnold, son of the composer Samuel Arnold, is a fast-moving thriller that reveals certain aspects of the taste of the time. The setting of the Piedmontese Alps of Italy offers ample opportunity for imaginative scenic design, while the characters, including aristocrats and peasants, present a fertile social mixture. The plot revolves around a secret marriage, from which there is a son who is being raised by peasants and is unaware of his aristocratic parentage. His father is believed drowned in a shipwreck, and his mother is about to be forced by her own mother into an unwanted marriage with an unsavory local baron. The latter has imprisoned his own wife and is about to finish her off. Most of this is tightly presented in the first scene of Act I. The remainder of this three-act opera involves the flight of the heroine and the confrontations of her husband, a rich Sicilian count and not at all dead, with the evil, unwanted suitor, the baron. Finally the lovers are reunited and the baron and his soldiers literally destroyed--at the dangerous "Devil's Bridge." There is a good bit of moralizing (especially to the child) about being truthful and sporadic idealizations of peasant life and its virtues (simplicity, honesty, moral strength, godliness, and so on) as opposed to the inherent evils of the aristocracy (excepting, of course, the hero and heroine). Although the characters tend to be stereotypic and without development or change and the ideas are cliché ridden, the action is rapid and suspenseful.

The music comprises an overture and nineteen songs and ensembles, of which Horn wrote a little more than half.[31] Of the vocal pieces there is one quartet, one trio, two choruses, three duets and thirteen solos. The result of the predominating strophic form of the songs, an unflagging use of major keys, and stark simplicity is one of sameness, relieved only by three pieces closer to a more complex Italian aria style. Two of these are by Braham and one by Horn. Some of the solos have a distinctly folk-like lilt, while a few, such as "Is there a heart that never loved" by Braham, hark back to the lyrical classicism of the late eighteenth century. The simplicity and charm Braham created in that particular song made it the "hit" of <u>The Devil's Bridge</u> and earned it great popularity in the first part of the century.[32] One may conclude that the success of the opera rested on the rapid pace of the plot, the direct charm of the music, and the ability of the performers. Horn, in fact, excelled in the leading part of Count Belino, making it one of his most distinctive roles when he later came to this country.

New York's Park Theater burned in 1820 (the same year as the Washington and Philadelphia theater fires) but was rebuilt the following year to hold 2,500 people. Although gas lighting had been installed in Philadelphia's New Theater in 1816, it took ten years before it appeared in New York. There the new building was lit by oil lamps hung in three large chandeliers and ample exits were provided, for besides its own recent history and that of Philadelphia, the Richmond fire cast a long shadow. According to critic Richard Grant White, the father of architect Stanford White, this was a bare, dreary place with rough benches, too closely modeled on the old building of 1798.[33]

Despite the modest accommodations, all classes and segments of society came for entertainment. By 1820 nineteen theaters in New York were more or less successfully offering their plays, comic operas, afterpieces, melodramas and other entertainments. Prostitutes and Afro-Americans had designated sections and entrances, liquor was available, and rowdiness was not uncommon. For the lengthy performances which began at 6:30 or 7:00 and lasted until close to midnight, the admission prices ranged from one dollar in the boxes to seventy-five cents for the pit and fifty cents for the gallery.[34]

SUBJECTS/SETTINGS

Several trends have become apparent in these operas that span the late eighteenth and early nineteenth centuries. The great value placed on family life, including its sacrifices and conflicts, ultimately rewarded or not, emerged as a major topic of serious librettos or comedies, pervaded by a strong moralistic tone. Patriotism, democratic views, the "simple virtues," and innate goodness often characterize a hero or become secondary themes of the plot. Settings tend to have the exotic tinge of a distant place or emphasize the surroundings of nature. These ideas and images were not confined to comic operas, but also appeared in fiction, poetry, plays, and the visual arts, reflecting the distinctive taste and atmosphere of the time.

Family life is a prime focus as the problems of parents or guardians, children, prospective marriages, and economic status arise to become the crux of the drama, as we have seen in the examples discussed. In some cases youth had to exert its new-found strength with parental authority and develop a more equal relationship, while in others a parent's manipulation had to be undone. Even Pocahontas in The Indian Princess, in the face of an unwanted marriage to the local Indian prince Miami, leads British forces to rescue her own choice of husband, the Englishman Rolf. Aristocrats are usually confined to castles or dungeons, generally viewed in an unfavorable light and sometimes finished off as in The Devil's Bridge. If age is seen as authoritarian and youth as self-determining, parents usually repent as all are reconciled and live happily ever after.

The moralistic tone is strong as evil gets its just reward. Sinful love emerges furtively, as in Bishop's Clari, but its true nature is recognized and rejected in favor of filial love and virtue. The devil offers Max a deal he cannot refuse in Der Freischütz: to sell his soul and win his beloved. Although Samiel seduces Max and then double-crosses him, all ends well when the miraculous appearance of a holy hermit thwarts the devil and sets things right. Max is forgiven, with a year of penance, and good triumphs.

A strong, straightforward patriotism characterizes Patrick, the hero of The Poor Soldier, who considers fighting for his country the path to glory. The common man's innate goodness and humane generosity are given standards of Patrick's behavior, while truth and simplicity are underscored as virtues and underhanded manipulations and greed as evils. Likewise, Blondel's loyalty to his master with its strong undercurrent of patriotism is an important element of Richard, in fact the linchpin of the drama. The Naval Pillar had extolled our seamen, as did many others of a similar stripe. Such pieces were popular in theaters wherever the music was accessible and actors could sing it. The common man with his virtues and foibles had become a central figure for librettists of comic opera to replace the classical Greek and Roman heroes of mythology who reigned in Italian opera seria.

Time periods accordingly shifted to either the present and everyday life or a remote, but post-classical past. The setting of Harun-al-Rashid's Baghdad for The AEthiop explored the scenic possibilities of an exotic environment. In London it had been noted as a stage spectacle and here was advertised as "in a style of splendor never exceeded on the American stage."[35] Caphania's entrance on her barge, the scene in Baghdad's market place with its "goods from all nations," and the one at the "Top of the Catacomb" offer ample opportunity for imaginative, colorful effects.[36] Other performances of this type of spectacle à la Arabian Nights, such as The Forty Thieves seen at the Park in New York four years earlier, attest to their popularity. Contemporary in time, if distant geographically, were the exotic, sinister, Mediterranean pirates that peopled some operas we have noted toward the beginning of the century.

Richard Coeur-de-Lion dramatized the distant past of the twelfth century with its castles and battles in a gripping fashion. Lack of historical knowledge made that remote period all the more mysterious and attractive. Any known facts were often disregarded (Richard was actually ransomed rather than rescued by force) or simply faulty. While the exoticism of The Indian Princess was closer to home physically, it was as removed psychologically from the English-speaking population as Baghdad or twelfth-century Europe.

The natural landscapes that would become such an important feature of nineteenth-century American painting in the work of Thomas Doughty (1793-1856), Thomas Cole (1801-1848) and others, found a welcome home in stage sets. Pastoral surroundings frame The Poor Soldier, which has six of its eight scenes set in the countryside. These seem conventional and stiff, however, by comparison to the natural beauty of the green German forest, by turn ominous or sheltering, in Der Freischütz or the Alpine settings in The Devil's Bridge or even the bandits' mountains and caves in The Castle of Andalusia. A stormy ocean opens Storace's No Song, No Supper with "A view of the Sea on the Coast of Cornwall," similar to the opening scene of his opera The Haunted Tower.

Characters, plots, and points of view in many of the English plays seem very old-fashioned and naive, as indeed they are from the perspective of our own day. The major flaw, however, is in the quality rather than the subjects of the plays. Plots in general tend to wander, rely on stock, banal situations, and are often quite dull. Characters often mouth cliché-ridden lines and lack psychological dimension. Exceptions such as The Devil's Bridge are thus all the more striking. In this case the play, which is clear, tense, and full of action, was written by the son of the experienced comic opera composer Samuel Arnold. He doubtless learned from his father, and by virtue of his own talent was capable of creating the elements of a viable play. The Indian Princess is also of a better quality, but it was written by American dramatist James Nelson Barker, who wrote other plays as well as verse and was considered, along with William Dunlap, a major playwright of the time. Undoubtedly Der Freischütz owed its great popularity more to Weber's fine music than to Friedrich Kind's libretto, which, although passable if not great, was far better than those of the English comic operas.

CRITICS

At the turn of the century theatrical as well as literary criticism was usually written from the point of view of established rather than individual opinion. Frequently a critic was a member of the clergy, but even when he was not, a strong moralistic tone was expressed. Art or technique was considered less important than morality, accepted social customs and the method of presentation. The Beggar's Opera aroused concern by the second decade of the century because its characters lived outside of respectable society, laughed at conventional behavior, and the political order as they scorned punishment, prison and the judicial system. Although staged with some consistency, its immorality became the target of recurrent complaints as critics began to see it as dangerous rather than satirical. Perhaps it touched too close to social reality or social anxiety to be easily tolerated. By the same token Schiller's play Die Räuber (The Robbers), translated and staged by William Dunlap, was criticized as immoral because of the sympathetic presentation of the characters and the moral implications. Even the popular and later revered Shakespeare appeared in cleaned-up versions in America. The stage, musical and otherwise, may have been enjoyed, but it was little approved.

Literary critics writing in journals or magazines often

ignored the theater or, like the clergy, condemned it. An exception was the Mirror of Taste and Dramatic Censor of Philadelphia, which in 1810 identified the drama as "a powerful moral agent," concurring with the view of a few others, notably Dunlap.[37] In 1825 an anonymous critic, "Musæus," appeared, but not until the 1840s do we have consistent musical criticism by knowledgeable men such as Fry, White, and later Dwight.

CONCLUSION

English comic opera style clearly predominated in the North while French opéra-comique held sway in New Orleans. Although there were structural features that were similar, such as the use of spoken dialogue and short songs, the differences are striking. Most obvious is the language and its reflection of each society's "taste," customs, and political hierarchy. Equally important, the French tended to depend on the music as an integral dramatic element, which if removed took much of the tension and sense away from the play, whereas this is less often the case with the English opera. There one can more easily add or subtract pieces without disturbing the progress of the drama; such flexibility could allow for more alterations in performances. Opéra-comique also more often interspersed dances and short descriptive orchestral pieces for color and a change of pace, just as had been done in other types of French opera. By the beginning of the nineteenth century both English and French comic opera had left their humble beginnings and acquired enough sophistication to make them attractive to a broad audience. The musical quality of the French opera was unquestionably better than that of the English, but history has decreed that only a very few of either would survive. Those musical entertainments were what was available, and our audiences, as a whole uncritical compared to those of European capitals, approved what they enjoyed and went back for more of the same or booed off the stage what they disliked. Criticism or affirmation was quick and direct.

The operatic scene would take on an added dimension in 1825 with Manuel Garcia's New York presentation of Rossini's

Barber of Seville (in Italian) and a repertory of nine other Italian works. That season of Italian opera marked the beginning of sporadic efforts to stage Italian opera in the original language. Eventually this more formal style would present a substantial challenge to the English opera's "play with music" format. Garcia's productions also marked the shift of the musical center away from Philadelphia to New York which, by 1820, had the largest population of any city in the United States. The death of the last of Philadelphia's vigorous musical leaders, Rayner Taylor in 1825 and Benjamin Carr in 1831, completed the shift to New York.

NOTES

1. Anne McClenny Krauss, "Alexander Reinagle, His Family Background and Early Professional Career," American Music IV/4 (1986), pp. 425-456.

2. George Thomson, A Select Collection of Original Scottish Airs, with arrangements by Pleyel, Haydn, Beethoven, Weber, and other contemporaries, is one of the better known.

3. Susan L. Porter, "English-American Interaction in American Musical Theater at the turn of the Nineteenth century," American Music IV/I (1986), p. 16.

4. David Grimsted, Melodrama Unveiled: American Theater and Culture 1800-1850 (Chicago: University of Chicago Press, 1968), p. 27. Chapter 2 has a detailed discussion of these attitudes. He notes a certain subtle rivalry for the individual's time and money as existing between church and theater.

5. Otto E. Albrecht, "Opera in Philadelphia, 1800-1830," Journal of the American Musicological Society, XXXII/3 (Fall 1979), p. 499.

6. Michael R. Turner, ed., The Parlour Song Book: A Casquet of Vocal Gems (New York: The Viking Press, 1972), p. 143.

7. Nicholas Temperley, ed., Music in Britain: The Romantic Age 1800-1914 (London: The Athlone Press, 1981), p. 301.

8. Stephen Storace, No Song, No Supper, Musica Britannica, Vol. XVI (London: Stainer & Bell, 1951-; 2nd ed., 1954-); Foreword by Roger Fiske.

9. Temperley, Music in Britain, p. 302.

10. Victor Fell Yellin, "Rayner Taylor," American Music, I/3 (1983), pp. 48-71; "Rayner Taylor's Music for The AEthiop: Part 1, Performance History," American Music, IV/1 (1986), pp. 249-267; and "Rayner Taylor's Music for The AEthiop: Part 2, The Keyboard Score (The Ethiop) and Its Orchestral Restoration," American Music, V/1 (1987), pp. 20-47. Recorded selections from The AEthiop are on New World Records 232 with notes by Yellin.

11. Henry Arnold Kmen, Music in New Orleans: The Formative Years 1791-1841 (Baton Rouge: Louisiana State University Press, 1966), p. 90.

12. Ibid., p. 74.

13. Ibid., pp. 232-233.

14. Ibid. p. 63, but without documentation on Adams. Oscar G. T. Sonneck, "The Musical Side of Our First Presidents," in Suum Cuique: Essays in Music (New York: G. Schirmer, 1916), p. 38, notes that Adams, although less musically inclined than other Presidents, had a very positive reaction to Grétry's Le Jugement de Midas at The Hague in 1782.

15. Stephen Willier, "Early Nineteenth-Century Opera and the Impact on the Gothic" (Ph.D. dissertation, University of Illinois, Urbana-Champaign, 1987).

16. David Charlton, Grétry and the Growth of Opéra-Comique (Cambridge: Cambridge University Press, 1986); Patrick J. Smith, The Tenth Muse: A Historical Study of the Opera Libretto (New York: Schirmer Books, 1975).

17. Kmen, Music in New Orleans, p. 84.

18. The term "season" throughout the century referred to anything from three or four performances in a week to many spread out over several months.

19. John Curtis,"One Hundred Years of Grand Opera in Philadelphia," (Unpublished typescript at the Historical Society of Pennsylvania in Philadelphia), p. 56.

20. Henry Placide, the oldest son, became a well-known actor, while another son, Thomas, acted in New York and Philadelphia. Daughters Jane and Caroline acted respectively in New Orleans and Charleston.

21. W. Stanley Hoole, The Ante-Bellum Charleston Theatre (Tuscaloosa: University of Alabama Press, 1946), pp. 79-91.

22. Yellin and Johnson have suggested, referring to different events, that the many theater fires and the amount of material lost and not consistently replaced influenced the waning of English opera as entertainment.

23. Oscar G. T. Sonneck, *Early Opera in America* (New York: G. Schirmer, 1963), Chapter 2.

24. Katherine Hines Mahan, "History of Music in Columbus Georgia 1828-1928" (Ph.D. dissertation, Florida State University, 1967), p. 11.

25. William Craig Winden, "The Life and Music Theater Works Of John Hill Hewitt" (DMA dissertation, University of Illinois, Champaign-Urbana, 1972), pp. 21-23.

26. Sonneck, *Early Opera in America*, p. 118.

27. William B. Wood, *Personal Recollections of the Stage* (Philadelphia, 1855), pp.237-238.

28. Michael Kelly, *Reminiscences*, ed. Roger Fiske (London: Oxford University Press, 1975), p. xix.

29. H. Wiley Hitchcock, "An Early American Melodrama," *Notes* XII (1955), pp.375-388; James Nelson Barker and John Bray, *The Indian Princess*, in *Earlier American Music* 11 (New York: Da Capo Press, 1972).

30. Curtis, "One Hundred Years," p. 55.

31. Charles Edward Horn, *The Devil's Bridge*. Score printed by Goulding of London in Library of Congress, libretto in Van Pelt Library, University of Pennsylvania.

32. Charles Hamm, *Yesterdays: Popular Song in America* (New York: W. W. Norton & Co., 1979), p. 164.

33. Peter George Buckley, "To The Opera House: Culture and Society in New York City 1820-1860" (Ph. D. dissertation, State University of New York at Stony Brook, 1984), pp. 101-102.

34. Ibid., pp. 102-103.

35. Yellin, "Rayner Taylor's Music for *The AEthiop*: Part 1, Performance History," p. 263.

36. *The AEthiop* score is in the Harvard Library Collection. A photo copy was kindly lent me by Martha Schleifer.

37. William Charvat, *The Origins of American Critical Thought 1810-1835* (New York: Russell & Russell, 1968).

3

English and "Englished" Opera: 1825–1847

All songs of current lands come sounding round me,
The German airs of friendship, wine and love,
Irish ballads, merry jigs and dances, English warbles,
Chansons of France, Scotch tunes, and o'er the rest,
Italia's peerless compositions.
Across the stage with pallor on her face, yet lurid passion,
Stalks Norma brandishing the dagger in her hand.
I see poor crazed Lucia's eyes' unnatural gleam,
Her hair down her back falls loose and dishevel'd.

Walt Whitman
from Proud Music of the Storm

THE BACKDROP

While Philadelphia still treasured its label as the "Athens of America," by 1820 New York had emerged as a city where business held the preeminent place. In 1825 the Erie Canal was completed, connecting New York's business community with the Great Lakes region, and for the next twelve years a relatively stable economy prevailed.[1] The populations of each city, about 200,000, would increase with the slow shift from rural to urban areas as developing industrialization and factory production created jobs. The resulting economic upheavals for the urban poor contrasted sharply with the stability of a richer group that, by the 1820s, was wealthy even by European standards. This economic disparity disturbed the prevailing egalitarian ideal of Jacksonian America.

That ideal was articulated during the campaign of 1828 in a call (at that time not unfamiliar) "against aristocracy, privilege, and government interference with a providential order . . . for the simple, the natural, the just."[2] The emphasis on man's equality, individuality, and a natural order would linger for some time to permeate all attitudes and prejudices, including those toward theater and opera.

Those art forms continued to arouse suspicion in religious groups and their leaders, who recognized the potential propaganda power of the stage. Although the serious churchgoer could hardly visit the theater and maintain a clear conscience, a persistent view held by nonreligious critics envisioned the theater and opera as a possible vehicle for educational benefit and moral uplift. Walt Whitman reflected this persistent if minority opinion when he observed: "All--every age and every condition in life--may with profit visit a well-regulated dramatic establishment, and go away better than when they came."[3] In New Orleans and the South, where attitudes were somewhat less rigid, there was less animosity toward the theater.[4]

Foremost among social concerns in the 1830s was a mounting spirit of reform and a general support for education and "improvement." Dorothy Dix bent her energies toward the just treatment of criminals and the insane and published her landmark book, <u>Prisons and Prison Discipline</u>, in 1845. In Massachusetts Josiah Holbrook founded a system of adult education, the "American Lyceum," so popular that it spawned close to one hundred branches in the next two years.[5] A number of institutions of higher learning as diverse as Mount Holyoke College (1836), and the University of Notre Dame (1843) appeared within a decade, while in Boston Lowell Mason founded an Academy of Music for the education of musicians. In the early 1830s Mason had convinced private, and later public, schools in Boston to establish music education classes on the basis that learning to read music developed intellectual discipline, and that singing was physically and psychologically beneficial.[6]

One of the great economic depressions of the century took hold from 1837-1843 with fluctuations and slow recovery by the mid-forties. In New York the Park Theater's response to the economic crunch was to add the best actors available to its company, but even this helped little.[7] Only the "novelties," the critic wailed, could fill theaters in these hard times, but that was a slight exaggeration.

ENGLISH TRANSLATIONS AND ARRANGEMENTS

To the popular repertory of operas in English a number of new translations (often referred to as "Englished") were added in the late 1820s and early 1830s. Works by English composers included Arne's Artaxerxes in florid Italian style, Bishop's Guy Mannering, derived from the Sir Walter Scott novel and Lacy's two pasticcios, Cinderella and The Maid of Judah. This last was based on Scott's novel Ivanhoe and took music from Rossini's opera Mosè in Egitto (Moses in Egypt). Cinderella used music from Rossini's own Cenerentola (Cinderella) and his Armida, Guillaume Tell (William Tell), and Maometto II. Rossini was now one of the most popular and often-performed opera composers in Europe. Translations, or "Englished" works, newly added to the repertory consisted of Weber's Abu Hassan, Boieldieu's La Dame blanche (The White Lady adapted by American author John Howard Payne), Auber's La Muette de Portici (The Dumb Girl of Portici) and Mozart's The Magic Flute in Charles Horn's arrangement. The translations of Cinderella, The Barber of Seville, Der Freischütz, The Marriage of Figaro and, a bit later, La sonnambula (The Sleepwalker) attained exceptional popularity often because of the performance of a celebrity. Horn's fine acting did much to popularize Der Freischütz, Maria Malibran enchanted audiences as Rosina in Barber of Seville in Italian, and the Woods created a great hit in the English version of La sonnambula. Charles Horn's collaboration with John Braham in writing The Devil's Bridge, or The Piedmontese Alps, which had established Horn's reputation in England as a first-class composer, became a perennial favorite as we have noted. When Horn immigrated here, he became a major figure for a number of years in the production of English language opera and concerts.

Charles Edward Horn (1786-1849), influential as a singer,

composer, manager, and eventually publisher, arrived in New York in 1827. He opened at the Park Theater on July 20 as Seraskier, one of his famous roles, in Storace's popular "rescue" opera, Siege of Belgrade, followed several months later by his highly successful characterization of Caspar in Weber's Freischütz. Horn had studied singing with the well-known singer Venanzio Rauzzini (1746-1810), the teacher of Nancy Storace and John Braham, who became one of the finest tenors of the time. Horn and John Sinclair, who also later came to America, appeared together as leading singers in Bishop's opera Aladdin at Drury Lane when Braham was music director there. Horn could encompass both tenor and baritone roles, had played double bass in the orchestra at Covent Garden, conducted the orchestra at Royal Gardens, "one of the finest orchestras in Europe" and, by the time he came to New York, had composed about twelve operas as well as songs, glees, two oratorios, and other works.[8] Clearly an accomplished, versatile musician, he wrote five more operas in America, but was known primarily, until he lost his voice in 1833, as a singer or arranger. He made English versions of Barber of Seville, La Cenerentola, Der Freischütz, and The Magic Flute, among others, simplifying the orchestration to accommodate instrumentalists less able than their European counterparts. Horn's alterations of originals, no matter how disfiguring, helped expand the vogue for Weber and accelerate the popularization of Rossini and Mozart. His version of Cinderella elicited a recurrent plea expressed in the New York Mirror (December 22, 1832) that such performances would banish foreign-language opera, although at that time it seemed hardly a threat. Horn actively promoted English ballad operas, works of Storace, Bishop, Arne, and especially his own. Earlier in London he had been a teacher of Michael Balfe (1808-1870), the composer of numerous operas that would become popular in America, notably The Bohemian Girl. As a dynamic performer Horn not only set standards by his excellent singing and acting, but also introduced and promoted first-class music.

Other singers, mainly English, who attracted critical acclaim for their performances included Mrs. Austin, famous in Cinderella and greatly admired by the Mirror's critic; Miss Hughes, also noted for Cinderella and her role in the English Freischütz; Mme. Feron;

and Mrs. Knight. Popular male singers were Horn's former London colleague John Sinclair, for whom Rossini had written the part of Idreno in his opera seria Semiramide, and John Jones, a composer and singer. A husband and wife team, Mr. and Mrs. Wood, promoted English operas and English translations in two sojourns here, the first from 1833-1836 and the second a brief four-month stay in 1840-1841. Another English couple, the Seguins, who would almost monopolize English opera during the 1840s, made a more lasting impact. Many of these singers came with strong London reputations and extensive experience.

Rossini's La Cenerentola had been made into an extremely successful pasticcio in London in 1830 by Rophino Lacy, who took music from the original and three other Rossini operas, Armida, Guillaume Tell, and Maometto II, to create Cinderella, or the Fairy Queen and the Little Glass Slipper. Because all of the music was by the same composer with alterations kept to a minimum, this was an unusual pasticcio, much more consistent and of a higher quality than most. Lacy changed the unfamiliar elements of Rossini's plot into the fairy tale familiar to English audiences to help ensure success. And successful it was, as we know from its many performances on both sides of the Atlantic and the publications of the music in both London and New York.[9] The star was English soprano Mrs. Elizabeth Austin, a "marvelous beauty" with "an exquisite voice" who specialized in opera adaptions in English and had sung in London at Drury Lane.[10] After the arrival of London stars Mr. and Mrs. Wood in 1833, Mrs. Austin's popularity became less secure and in 1835, although still highly acclaimed, she and her male companion, F. H. F. Berkeley, returned to England. The beautiful lady was not married to Berkeley, and this inevitably would have had an adverse effect on her image.

Before Garcia's performances, audiences had seen major European operas only as translated, dim distortions of the originals. Restructured plots and selected music (usually with changes) from a few Mozart and Rossini works were known mainly through the English translations and "arrangements" of Henry Bishop. In his version of Don Giovanni, called Don Juan, or The Libertine (London 1817, Philadelphia 1827), most of the ensembles were omitted, most of the arias changed or deleted, and a duet from The

Magic Flute inserted along with some dances by Mozart, Martini, and Bishop himself.[11] Bishop's version of The Marriage of Figaro (London 1819, New York 1823) underwent similar surgery, as did The Barber of Seville (London 1818, New York 1819). Bishop was not quite as artistically insensitive as one might conclude from this mangling of Mozart and Rossini. He was continuing the common and expedient British custom, encouraged or required by London's theatrical managers, of translating and adapting foreign language operas for London performances. This hardly excuses the custom or its sometimes grotesque results, but it was a common practice, and the notion that one should faithfully reproduce the composer's intentions was barely on the horizon. Many of the arranged pieces with their distortions, euphemistically labeled "improvements," were then brought to this country by managers and performers. A notable example was Weber's Der Freischütz, which flourished here probably in both Bishop's and Horn's versions. Two other Weber successes were Abu Hassan, a one-act comedy, and the three-act Oberon (set originally to an English libretto). For the latter, John Braham and Mrs. Wood had created the leading roles in 1826 at Covent Garden in London.

OTHER TYPES OF THEATER

Because operas were so intermingled with other types of theater, one needs to have a general idea of what those productions were. Favorite dramas were the standard Shakespearean plays, often with some music, in particular Hamlet, King Lear, and Richard III. These could be depended on to draw large audiences, especially if illuminated by a famous star such as Edwin Forrest. Despite the Shakespearean repertory's status as "classic" with the American public, it was subject to cuts, deletions, and broad censoring of sections considered immoral or in some way unsuitable for audiences. Contemporary spoken plays, again often with music, would include Kotzebue's Pizarro or Sheridan's School for Scandal, for example. Lighter melodramas by Pocock (Rob Roy) or Colman (Mountaineers), used inserted songs and background music to enhance action and atmospheric effects.

Standard afterpieces such as Arnold's The Spoiled Child or Shield's The Poor Soldier could still be relied on to help fill a theater. Entertainments in general ran the gamut from the successful, if lowbrow, spectacle The Cataract of the Ganges to the sophistication of Der Freischütz.[12] Often a viable work, then as now, appeared in several guises. For example, Scott's popular poem Lady of the Lake became a play, then Rossini's opera, in both French and Italian versions, and may have even had other lives.

In the late twentieth century, a time of relatively standardized musical and theatrical performances, it is difficult to imagine the amount of improvisations and alterations that were a way of life 175 or so years ago. This, however, seems to be one of the most important features of theatrical production at that time, for as we have noted, performances varied not only with changing casts, but also with the musical cuts, interpolations, and arrangements that reflected the taste and abilities of both music director and performers. From a practical point of view it is important to consider that performers were expected to know a very large number of roles, were given little time in which to learn them, and often had few rehearsals. Improvisation was an essential survival tactic, and if you had not had time to learn all the new songs in an opera you could be fairly sure that the audience would not object to hearing something they already knew and liked.

GARCIA'S SEASON

Considering the prevalence of English opera, Manuel Garcia's appearance with his Italian repertory and company in November 1825 at New York's most prestigious theater, the Park, was dramatic and challenging. His productions of Italian opera, replete with its elaborate, highly sophisticated music performed by thoroughly professional singers and instrumentalists, contrasted sharply with the less formal English opera's "play-with-music" format enacted by actor-singers. In addition, a sense of elitism, exclusivity, and mystery was added to the musical magic of a Rossini or Mozart by the foreign-language cloak that obscured the plot. The audience, instructed as to dress and deportment by the newspapers, consisted of New York's rich and fashionable. Royalty and intelligentsia were represented by Joseph Bonaparte, the former king of Spain, Lorenzo da Ponte, poet and librettist, James Fenimore Cooper, whose best-selling novel The Last of the Mohicans would be published the following year, and others. Garcia followed his opening Barber of Seville by a season of Italian operas selected on the basis of their current popularity abroad. Because Rossini was the rage in London, the repertory was weighted in his favor. Audiences responded positively to the style and quality of performance in the composer's Tancredi, Otello, Il turco in Italia (The Turk in Italy), La Cenerentola, and Mozart's Don Giovanni. These masterpieces added a new dimension to the operatic scene, and although Garcia never toured even to musically sophisticated Philadelphia, many Philadelphians came to hear his company in New York.[13]

In the opening performance the orchestra of carefully selected instrumentalists performed with impressive skill.[14] The singing was superior, notably that of Garcia's seventeen-year-old daughter Maria who, rigorously trained by her father, had already made a successful debut in London and would soon achieve extraordinary fame in Europe as Maria Malibran (1808-1836). Garcia himself (1775-1832) was an internationally famous singer. Of a dynamic and fiery personality, he had created the role of Almaviva under Rossini himself in the 1816 Rome premiere of Barber of Seville, was sought after and highly regarded in the finest opera houses of Naples, Paris, and London and was one of the best paid tenors of his time. By his late forties he was in London, declining vocally (a distinct throb had appeared, and the volume had lessened), embroiled in altercations with theater managers and ready to seek new, less critical audiences.[15] In the fall of 1825 Dominick Lynch, an emissary of the Park Theater's manager Stephen Price, had arrived in London looking for an opera troupe to import. Lynch, an amateur musician and enthusiastic patron of music active in the recently restructured Philharmonic Society, especially enjoyed opera.[16] Garcia responded favorably to the optimistic, rosy report of America's eagerness for Italian opera and agreed to bring his company (consisting mainly of his family) to New York.

Although initially popular because of its novelty and Maria Garcia's appeal, the Italian opera gradually began to lose its audience. After ten months and eighty performances, having earned a gross of $56,685, Garcia and most of his company left for Mexico.[17] Initial interest in this foreign divertissment had waned, but the significance of Garcia's single ten-month operatic season was twofold. First, the high quality (by American standards) of performances by experienced, professionally-trained singers supported by a competent orchestra and second, the staging of major works in a form close to the originals. The subtlety, informed sophistication, and technical demands of an aria such as "Una voce poco fa" (The Barber of Seville) stand at the other end of the spectrum from the stark simplicity, at times crudity, of songs from the widely popular ballad operas. Considering the usual English language repertory, surprisingly few criticisms were initially raised concerning the use of Italian. One suspects that the sophistication of the music and performance overcame any criticism regarding the use of a foreign language.

As "the magnet who attracted all eyes and won all hearts," Maria Garcia's charismatic quality became one of the main sources of the troupe's success.[18] Her convincing acting, as well as her musical expressivity and mastery of the difficult vocal technique required for the Rossini and Mozart repertory, won dramatically positive responses from audiences. Affectionately nicknamed the "Signorina" by her public, Maria's sweet face with the lovely dark eyes indicate little of her inner force and determination. Soon, in European capitals, she would be recognized as one of the finest interpreters of Rossini and Bellini of her generation. Her early death at age twenty-eight may well have contributed to the legend that grew up around her name. Soon after her debut in New York she married a forty-four year old merchant Eugène Malibran, perhaps to escape her father's controlling domination. She remained in New York when the Garcia company departed for Mexico, to sing at the Grace Church and subsequently the newly built Bowery Theater managed by Charles Gilfert, formerly of Richmond and Charleston. There she appeared in some of the popular English works (Horn's Devil's Bridge and Arne's Love in a Village), as well as Don Giovanni and, finally, an English translation of Boieldieu's Jean de Paris introduced several months earlier by the New Orleans company in French. The public found Maria's accented English charming. Then, having gained her professional experience in the operatic provinces of America, she left for Paris, the opera capital of the world, to achieve lasting fame as one of the greatest singers of the century.

THE FRENCH OPERA COMPANY

In July of 1827 the French Opera Company from New Orleans, under the direction of John Davis, opened its first six-month northern tour at the Park Theater in New York. A distinguishing feature of this company was that it employed seasoned singers, musicians, and dancers imported from Paris. Equally important, their astute manager was by now thoroughly experienced from his ten seasons of opera in New Orleans. To top it off the troupe had a strong, successful French repertory that included, besides the new hit, Boieldieu's La Dame blanche, works of Auber, Dalayrac, Isouard, Cherubini, and other well-known contemporary French composers. The purpose of Davis' northern tour was to escape the two-edged sword of falling box office receipts and ensuing loss of members of the company. The heat of the New Orleans summer coupled with recurrent yellow fever epidemics discouraged theater attendance and often caused his performers to disband. A tour offered fresh audiences, steady income, continued employment and hence a means of maintaining his company intact. The opening double bill of Isouard's Cendrillon (Cinderella again) and Dalayrac's Maison à vendre (House for Sale) prefaced about forty operas that were staged over the next two months in Philadelphia as well as New York.

Boieldieu's hit, La Dame blanche, premiered in Paris in 1825, was based on a combination of ideas from Sir Walter Scott's novels, notably Guy Mannering and The Monastery.[19] Librettist Eugène Scribe, famous for his texts for many contemporary French composers, especially Meyerbeer, cleverly wove threads from these novels into a new drama. Scott was not only a tremendously popular novelist during the nineteenth century, but also a highly favored source for composers of opera. Besides the well-known Lucia di Lammermoor based on The Bride of Lammermoor and Rossini's La donna del lago (The Lady of the Lake) there were many others.[20] La Dame blanche, one of the most popular operas of the century, had received 1,000 performances in Paris by 1862 and been translated and staged all over Europe. Romantic elements commonly found in nineteenth-century opera, among them a touch of the supernatural, a chateau partly in ruins, an old family servant full of nostalgic dreams, picturesque peasants, a young man searching for his parents and past, and the triumph of love over class differences, weave a drama that appealed strongly to the audience of its time. Boieldieu's music, although harmonically conservative, has considerable melodic grace and orchestral color and manages to work in several Scottish tunes for atmosphere. As a testament to the music's viability, three of the tenor arias still appear on concert programs.

The New Orleans company offered New York and Philadelphia sixty performances of thirty-two operas by fourteen composers. The New York American exulted: "This company is as good as those heard in the provinces of France and superior to those heard in the Capitals of Europe outside France."[21] New Orleans papers were similarly adulatory when the troupe returned home. During John Davis's six summer tours in the North (the last was in 1833), the most popular composers were Boieldieu with seven operas staged and Auber with an equal number. Most frequent productions were La Dame blanche, Der Freischütz, deceptively translated as in Paris as Robin des bois (Robin of the Woods), and The Barber of Seville, in French of course.[22] This exposure to such a consistently superior series of French performances enhanced the opera seasons of New York and Philadelphia, as the variety, quantity, and fine quality expanded the audience's experience, raising the general level of expectations and taste.

DA PONTE'S INFLUENCE

Lorenzo da Ponte (1749-1838) was one of Mozart's librettists and a figure of some importance in opera's general development. Originally from Venice, this accomplished, versatile writer, who saw himself as primarily a poet, had become a much sought-after librettist in Vienna, subsequently spent a period as a theater librettist in London and eventually settled in New York in 1805. His reaction to the New Orleans company reflected the traditional Italian impatience with French music, but he was enthusiastic about the Garcia company. When he went to greet Garcia and identified himself as the librettist of Don Giovanni, Garcia was reputed to have responded by singing the opening of the opera's "Champagne" aria to him.[23] Da Ponte, now a teacher of Italian and a dealer in imported books, enthusiastically promoted Garcia's performances by attending them with his students, as well as printing and selling the libretto of Don Giovanni in English and Italian.[24] He followed his unsuccessful attempt to produce Italian opera in 1830 by eventual collaboration with Giovanni Montressor, a tenor and impresario from Italy. In 1832 the two initiated, with Rossini's La Cenerentola (a dependable choice in any language), a season of Italian opera at the Richmond Hill Theater, soon renamed the Italian Opera House. This fulfilled in part the energetic da Ponte's long cherished dream of personally bringing Italian culture to New York. What better medium than opera in which he himself had achieved such great success (albeit thirty-nine years before) and which the city had already had a taste of in Garcia's productions. Richmond Hill's season ran from October 6, 1832, through May 11, 1833, with more than fifty performances, including a tour to Philadelphia. Despite a fair company, good reviews and weak competition from the current English opera, the enterprise lost money. Both da Ponte and Montressor were left with bad feelings and large debts. On the positive side, the company had premiered Rossini's L'inganno felice (The Happy Deception) and L'Italiana in Algeri (The Italian Woman in Algiers), Bellini's Il pirata (The Pirate), and Mercadante's Elisa e Claudio, all contemporary and successful in European theaters.

Undaunted by this financial failure, da Ponte now undertook

to raise money for the construction of a theater specifically for opera. This separation of opera from the other types of stage entertainment with which it had previously been housed, would, he hoped, give it a stronger identity and a more permanent basis. It also replicated the European system he knew so well. Support from wealthy citizens with strong cultural interests such as Philip Hone, a former mayor of the city, and his friend Dominick Lynch, resulted in the construction of the Italian Opera House. It was described thus:

The auditorium was different in arrangement than any hitherto seen in America. The second tier was composed entirely of private boxes, hung with curtains of crimson silk; . . . The whole interior was pronounced magnificent, and the scenery and curtains were beautiful beyond all precedent. The ground of the front-boxes was white, with emblematical medallions and octagonal panels of crimson, blue, and gold. The dome was painted with representations of the Muses. The sofas and pit-seats were covered with damask, and the floors were all carpeted.[25]

With da Ponte and his friend Rivafinoli as managers for the first six months the financial basis proved totally impractical and doomed to failure.

Philip Hone noted in his diary in November of 1835 that two elements worked together to oppose the acceptance of Italian opera: one was the use of a foreign language and the other the aristocratic atmosphere that the boxes induced. Although undoubtedly true at the time, these were the very elements that eventually gained support for opera from those socially elite elements, of which Hone was one, seeking class symbols. Hone then added that "the immense houses which Mr. and Mrs. Wood bring nightly to the Park, prove that the New Yorkers are not devoid of musical taste, notwithstanding that the Italian opera does not succeed." In a word, there was no reason for Italian opera to exist, especially in the face of a successful English opera that flourished unconcerned with attempts to establish foreign-language performances, in Italian or French.

NEW YORK

The Mr. and Mrs. Wood whom Hone mentions had arrived in New York from London in 1832 and would become particularly well known for their performances of Bellini's La sonnambula in English. The first time they presented the opera in Philadelphia its enthusiastic reception gave it a run of fourteen nights. Mrs. Wood, the former Mary Ann Paton of Scottish extraction, had performed in concerts as a child prodigy and at twenty had debuted at the Haymarket Theater in The Marriage of Figaro. She also sang Italian opera in London and was described as having a brilliant vocal technique, fine taste and musicality, as well as a beautiful, expressive face. She met her handsome future husband, while both were singing at Covent Garden. He had been reputedly trained by James Maeder (later to marry American actress Clara Fisher) and possessed a strong tenor that apparently combined some of the virtues of his contemporaries, the "glowing strength of Bettini, and the soft delicate beauty of Salvi, with the flexibility and truth of Perelli."[26] His temper, however, was short and that embroiled him and his wife in at least two unfortunate theatrical disputes in New York and Boston.[27] Besides La sonnambula, the Woods' other big attraction was the ever popular Cinderella by Lacy. In the fall of 1833 they staged twenty works of ballad and grand operas in Philadelphia at the Chestnut Street Theater including Love in a Village, Masaniello, Der Freischütz, Fra Diavolo, Cinderella, Duenna, The Devil's Bridge, The Quaker, and The Maid of Judah. At their last performance in Philadelphia, late in 1840, they sang in a truly fine production of Norma in an English translation by Joseph Fry, brother of composer William Henry Fry (1813-1864). The latter directed the music.[28] Mrs. Wood was an authoritative performer with a "rich and powerful voice...[of] great facility."[29]

La sonnambula, a work of the sentimental, semi-serious genre, was one of the most popular operas of the nineteenth century in America, first in English and later in Italian. Bellini, ever seeking the ideal phrases for his musical imagination, compelled his librettist Felice Romani (1788-1865), one of Italy's finest poets, to rewrite the final cabaletta "Ah, non giunge" ten times before he was satisfied.[30] The leading roles were created specifically for two of the most famous singers of the day, Giuditta Pasta and Giovanni Rubini. Premiered in Milan in 1831, La sonnambula was later sung by Maria Malibran in English in London under the composer's direction, to great acclaim, and in 1835 performed by Mr. and Mrs. Wood and the stock company at the Park Theater in New York. It became as popular as Cinderella, and the Woods outdid themselves in the leading roles. Nine years later Palmo's theater staged it in Italian, and in 1857 it was chosen to open the season at the Academy of Music in New York under conductor Carl Anschütz. Partly because of its small cast, three main roles, and three lesser ones who sing mainly in the ensembles, La sonnambula was ideal for travel and became a staple ingredient of touring and stock companies. Moreover, its highly successful parodies, The Roof Scrambler done at the National Theater in 1837 and an "Ethiopian Burlesque" version, Lo! som am de beauties, done at Palmo's in 1845, brought it to a much wider social group.

The setting is a Swiss village and the plot concerns the marriage of Amina, an adopted orphan, to Elvino, a wealthy peasant. This happy event is almost thwarted by the misplaced jealousy of the husband-to-be and the provocative if innocent sleepwalking of his beloved. A disguised count returning to his nearby castle is the object of the hero's suspicions (the heroine in her sleepwalking mode gets into the count's bed at one point), and a dread phantom in white, which turns out to be the sleepwalking heroine, roams the village after dark. Bellini's exquisite music, as it spins out highly ornamented melodic lines that forcefully activate the text, concentrates on the beauty of the voice more than the character or the drama. Simplicity of accompaniment places the singer at center stage as it underlines the warmth and color of the vocal line. According to Richard Grant White:

> La sonnambula was the delight of all music-loving people, cultivated and uncultivated, from North to South, from East to -- but then there was no West. Nothing but "Still so gently o'er me stealing," or "Hear me swear, now," was heard from the throats of singers, the fingers of piano-forte thrummers, and even the lips of whistlers; for never before was there

such a pathetic puckering.[31]

In 1836 the Italian Opera House, following a second disastrous attempt at producing Italian opera, became the National Theater with a repertory expanded beyond opera. In 1839, one year after da Ponte's death, the National Theater burned down, and in 1840 Stephen Price, the enterprising manager of the Park Theater who had originally commissioned Dominick Lynch to seek an opera company in London, died. An era had ended. Da Ponte had labored long and determinedly to bring Italian opera to America, and despite the many obstacles, problems, and failures he was crucial in its establishment. He was aided by a number of others, including Maria Malibran, America's first super-star prima donna who transfixed audiences, and certain essential background figures such as Price, Hone, and Lynch who respectively offered practical and financial support. During the next few years Italian opera performed in its native tongue would lie almost dormant, but flourish in English translations to win fervent followers as its music became well known and popular.

One of those background figures who promoted Italian opera was Ferdinand Palmo. Palmo, who had come to New York from Naples in 1815, became successful in the restaurant business and in 1841 opened an attractive establishment at 41 Chambers Street. In the following year he added an elaborately appointed concert hall on the second floor with "free nightly concerts." The happy combination of food and music flourished, and with the profits Palmo rebuilt the building next door (formerly Stoppani's Arcade Baths) into a beautifully decorated opera house with numbered seats, one price, and a requirement that ladies be accompanied by a gentleman. Thus the confusion of open seating was ended, and the admission of prostitutes controlled. The season ran from the beginning of February until the end of March and included, besides Bellini's I puritani (The Puritans), and Beatrice di Tenda, Donizetti's Belisario and Lucia. The star of the company, Eufrasia Borghese, had made her debut under the name of Bourgeois at the Paris Opéra-Comique in the French version of La Fille du régiment (The Daughter of the Regiment), written expressly for her by Donizetti. At Palmo's she was supported by a large orchestra and chorus under the direction of Michele Rapetti. The resulting cost of the operation sent Palmo, unfortunately, into bankruptcy by the end of the year.[32] As with da Ponte and many who would follow, Palmo had discovered the crushing expense of Italian opera, especially its singers.

The opera house, however, served other troupes, among them a German opera company in late 1845 and in the first months of 1847 an Italian Company headed by Sanquirico and Patti. Antonio Sanquirico was a comic singer who had debuted three years earlier at Palmo's, and tenor Salvatore Patti was the father of future singing star Adelina and her sisters Amalia and Carlotta, also fine singers. The company staged Donizetti's Linda di Chamounix for the first time with the beautiful, youthful prima donna Clotilda Barili (half-sister of the Patti daughters), as well as the first Verdi work to be heard here, I Lombardi alla prima crociata (The Lombards at the First Crusade), which was not well received, and Lucia.

THE SEGUINS AND FRY

Meanwhile English opera had been flourishing during the 1840s, mainly under the auspices of a new husband and wife team from England, Anne and Edward Seguin. Born in London in 1809, Edward Seguin, a bass, and his wife, soprano Anne Childe, had sung opera in London theaters before coming to New York in 1838. Edward opened in William Rooke's London hit of the previous year, Amilie, or The Love Test with Jane Shirreff in the title role and tenor John Wilson. Audiences and press were enthusiastic. The immensely popular Amilie was then taken by the Shirreff-Wilson company to other cities of the northern circuit including Boston, Washington, Baltimore, and Philadelphia.[33] Soon the Seguins formed their own opera troupe to stage operas in English. With the departure of the Shirreff-Wilson company and the Woods by 1841, the Sequins had little competition, and the continuing depression discouraged the entrance of new troupes from abroad. With their repertory of English translations the Seguins attracted a heterogeneous audience in smaller as well as larger cities and toured extensively. Their particular *tour de force* was Balfe's *The Bohemian Girl*, which they first presented on November 25, 1844, at the Park Theater. This work was acclaimed into this century and also achieved popularity in Europe, even winning France's coveted "Chevalier of the Legion of Honor" for its composer.

The Seguins' main repertory consisted of English versions of Italian works such as *Norma* and *Anne Boleyn*, both in translations by Joseph Fry, *I puritani*, *La sonnambula*, *The Elixir of Love*, *The Daughter of the Regiment*, *Fra Diavolo*, *Der Freischütz*, *The Barber of Seville*, *Amilie*, Horn's *The Maid of Saxony*, and others. Because the troupe traveled with only a few singers, it was dependent on members of the stock companies to fill in the minor parts. Over the years the repertory became too repetitious and worn, so that when competition arose in 1847 in Boston with Marti's Havana Opera Company, the Seguins fared poorly. Although they enlarged their troupe, hoping to compete more successfully, they never could regain their former popularity. They had, however, firmly paved the way for the Havana company by popularizing in English so much of that company's Italian repertory.

In 1845 the Seguins premiered the "first" American grand opera, William Henry Fry's *Leonora*, in Philadelphia at the Chestnut Street Theater on June 4. Written in the Italian style (that is, with sung recitatives, large vocal ensembles, and continuous music), Fry's opera reflects the influence of Bellini's *Norma*, a work that he knew intimately and admired. The libretto was written by Joseph Fry, William's brother, and based on *The Lady of Lyons* by Edward Bulwer-Lytton.

This play, the author's most popular, was first staged in New York on May 14, 1838, and became a staple of the dramatic repertory for many years. It was attractive to such a distinguished actor as William Charles Macready, who had created the leading role in London and also played it here. Joseph Fry shifted the time and place of the play from post-revolutionary France to sixteenth-century Spain and changed most of the characters, but retained the two main roles and the essentials of major events. The highly charged melodramatic plot has a proud, pure heroine, an evil, manipulative villain, and an honest but poor hero. Parental pressure is brought to bear when the heroine's father wants to alleviate his financial distress by having his daughter marry the wealthy villain, but--lo, the hero, formerly rejected as too poor and a peasant, now reappears, with financial means, to the rescue. The play's conflicts transferred to the opera concern the heroine's pride, which inhibits her from marrying someone of a lower social and economic caste even though she loves him, and her strong sense of filial duty, which nearly results in a loveless marriage for her. Because this is nineteenth-century America, justice happily triumphs as the poor hero at the end is wealthy, honored, and gets the heroine, who has seen the error of her ways.[34] Again we encounter some of the same flavorings frequently tasted in dramas, novels, and English operas of the period.

Fry's music, with its touches of Bellini, Donizetti, and Meyerbeer, is consistently competent and at times rises well above that. He came from a well-educated, sophisticated family, and although he pursued the profession of writer rather than musician, he had studied composition seriously with Leopold Meignen, a product of the Paris Conservatory, and was active in musical circles. Moreover, Fry had written two other operas prior to Leonora, so, while neither had been performed, he had thought about and worked with the special problems of the genre. In January of 1841 he and his brothers Joseph and Edward had staged an English version of Norma, a work he truly esteemed. His lyrical style and a proclivity for florid writing have been pointed out as signs of the influences of Bellini. The overture in particular has touches of Bellini while some of the choruses and ensembles are reminiscent of Donizetti.[35] Meyerbeer's shadow is evident in the more general structure of the French "grand opera" style, that is, the large orchestration and choruses, the frequent use of strong contrasts of a somewhat melodramatic nature, and a lengthy and contorted plot. Fry appears, in fact, no more eclectic or grandiose than Meyerbeer, but clearly far less musically gifted and skilled. It was hardly fair to compare Fry, whose vocation was not music, to composers such as Bellini or Donizetti, but that was the standard to which he was held. This was probably in part because he was such an enthusiastic champion of American opera, and in part because he was generally assertive and contentious.[36] White, an astute critic, observed in Fry an innate musical talent that might have been developed over time to produce fine works.[37] Unfortunately Fry died at fifty-one before that had taken place.

Leonora had the advantage of the Seguins singing the leading parts of Leonora and her father, Montalvo (a bass), while Mr. Frazer, a Scottish actor-singer who had joined the Seguin company the previous year, sang the tenor part of the hero, Julio. The production, heavily subsidized by Fry himself, was conducted by Adolf Schmidt, had a chorus of eighty and a large orchestra with a lot of percussion that even included an organ for the wedding scene. Although reviews from the press were mixed, Philadelphia audiences received the work with an enthusiasm that supported twelve performances, a large number of repetitions for that time. It was revived for four performances a year and a half later at the Walnut Street Theater and again in March 1858 in New York under conductor Carl Anschütz, but in an Italian translation. For the advocate of American opera and opera in English this must have seemed an ironic twist. At this time, however, most singers sang only in their native tongue, so it would have been unusual for an Italian company, such as this, to use English.

Unfortunately, the Seguin company did not include Leonora in their repertory of English operas, doubtless because it was impractical to hope that players in stock companies of the cities they visited would undertake such long and difficult parts. The large orchestral demands, however, may have been the greatest single deterrent. Impresario Max Maretzek commented in his Revelations some years later that if American operas, in which he includes Leonora, Arditi's The Spy, Bristow's Rip van Winkle, and his own Sleepy Hollow, had been premiered in Paris or London they would have gained favor here.[38] This seems a blatantly self-serving statement, but it has an element of truth, namely: works from abroad were automatically considered superior.

BOSTON AND NEW ENGLAND

Boston as the cultural leader of New England went

unmentioned in the last chapter because there icy prejudice against the theater melted only slowly. By 1825 thc influcncc of respected, and of course respectable, musicians such as the Graupners, the Ostinellis, and John Rowe Parker had modified disapproving attitudes, but female singers still needed a husband or father in close attendance, and change came slowly. Those who, from religious conviction, could not go to the theater could attend the concerts specifically planned for them that the singers of the theatrical company presented. There they would hear opera airs, including excerpts from works of Rossini, Weber, Mozart, and other Europeans. Those programs were also given on occasion in outlying towns such as Concord, Charleston, and Newburyport.[39]

By 1827 the Boston press had noted Charles Horn and Mrs. Knight in Guy Mannering and the popular Der Freischütz, Horn's specialty. John Davis and his New Orleans company presented their hit La Dame blanche with other works two years later. Soon Horn reappeared with the acclaimed Mrs. Austin when they achieved a good run in her tour de force, Cinderella. The following year she returned with Mr. Sinclair in, most notably, The Dumb Girl of Portici, Arne's Artaxerxes, Fra Diavolo, and John of Paris.

At the end of the same year the Woods first appeared in Boston to repeat the sure-fire Cinderella, along with such favorites as Love in a Village, The Barber of Seville, The Devil's Bridge, Guy Mannering, and The Marriage of Figaro. When they returned in October of 1835 after other engagements and a southern tour, they had added Meyerbeer's Robert the Devil and Bellini's La sonnambula to their repertory. The latter, at its American premiere in New York had been a great success. In fact a repetition in Boston of the much applauded La sonnambula helped smooth ruffled feelings when Mr. Wood again engaged in one of his more acrimonious and counterproductive exchanges with the press. The Woods returned to this country in 1840 to recapture some of their former fame, but only briefly, for by 1840 the depression had set in, the Seguins were now building a reputation, and Mr. Wood continued his destructive quarrels with the press.

NEW ORLEANS

Between his trips north from New Orleans during the summer months, John Davis fenced with competition from James Caldwell's company, falling receipts, and mounting expenses. Also periodic cholera epidemics, such as that of October 1832, devastated New Orleans and of course affected opera attendance adversely. Caldwell continued to import talent from Paris as well as new works such as *La Dame blanche*. That outstanding success, plus a French version of Weber's *Der Freischütz*, also strong at the box office, enabled Davis to get through the season. As he added major European operas to his repertory, he hired experienced singers to the company's roster. Spontini's *La Vestale* (*The Vestal Virgin*) and Méhul's *Joseph* were staged in 1828 and Rossini's *La Pie voleuse* (*The Thieving Magpie*) and *La Dame du Lac* in 1829. The Northern tours increased Davis's prestige at home as well as disseminating some of the new works. In the 1831 tour to New York and Philadelphia two highly acclaimed Auber works, *La Muette de Portici* (*The Dumb Girl of Portici*) and *Fra Diavolo*, were added to the repertory as well as Rossini's *Le Comte Ory* (*Count Ory*). The latter may have been less successful, for it was given fewer performances. These tours (the last was in 1833) also demonstrated Davis's considerable managerial skill, for his company of roughly fifty musicians and dancers traveled by road and river alternately, tolerated poor food and lodging, and put up with the many general discomforts associated with the primitive touring conditions of the time.

Meanwhile, Davis was not the only one to use tours. Caldwell's company went to Nashville, where he built a theater in the summer of 1825 and then proceeded on to Huntsville, Alabama. Two summers later he took his troupe to St. Louis for the first time and soon would venture as far as Cincinnati.

A realistic view of some performances of the time is gained from opinions of foreign visitors. In the spring of 1826, in New Orleans, *Der Freischütz* was announced for Caldwell's American Theater in Camp Street with high promises and fanfare by a "puff" in the local paper. After seeing the performance an English visitor complained that: "*Der Freischütz*, here metamorphosed into *The*

Wild Horseman of Bohemia. Six violins which played anything but music and some voices far from being human performed the opera which was applauded; the Kentuckians expressed their satisfaction in a hurrah, which made the very walls tremble."[40] The Wild Horseman returned the following year, one hopes with a more human voice that issued from Lydia Kelly, praised in both New York and London.[41]

Caldwell renovated the American Theater in 1828, turning it into a luxurious house with new carpeting, crimson upholstery, a beautifully painted dome with cut glass chandelier and seating for 2,000. The elegance of a theater, however, was not always duplicated in the manners of its audience, as is illustrated in the following comment of the Duke of Saxe-Weimar-Eisenach in his travel journal of 1825-1826.

> I found the boxes and the galleries thronged. In the pit there were few spectators, and these consisted of sailors and countrymen from Kentucky, who made themselves quite at ease on the benches, and cracked nuts during the finest pieces of music--a custom which I have noticed in all the English theaters [in the United States] and one from which my tobacco-chewing neighbors in the boxes did not refrain.[42]

Wealthier members of New Orleans society attended the theater as well as free African-Americans, for whom part of the third tier was set aside, Hispanics, and "sailors and countrymen." In order to control the more boisterous elements of his audience in the beautifully renovated theater, Caldwell hired his own security force. That, along with notices of theater regulations printed in the programs, seems to have been effective.

The theater renovation coincided with Caldwell's increasing dependence on "stars" and less on the cultivation of talent in the stock company. Higher paid stars of course meant lower pay for the stock company and a decline in quality of supporting players. As this practice became prevalent it would undermine and eventually destroy the stock company system.

One of his stars, Mrs. Edward Knight, debuted in January 1829 in Storace's The Haunted Tower, followed it up shortly with Love in a Village, and quickly won a strong following. This popular singer, already noted elsewhere, had made her debut at Drury Lane when she was fifteen, came to New York in 1826, was compared, as was everyone, to Malibran and would sing in cities of the East and South for the next twenty years. It is possible that she was part of Caldwell's stock company at one point, but in any case she returned consistently to New Orleans until 1836. Three years earlier she had replaced Jane Placide in the title role of Lacy's *Cinderella*, sung Susanna in *Marriage of Figaro* (probably Bishop's version) and the lead in an English version of Auber's *Fra Diavolo*, which had been popularized by Davis's company in French. John Sinclair came from New York to join her in *Love in a Village* and then in a revival of *Cinderella* in 1834. Soon, however, the Cinderella of the American premiere, Mrs. Austin, joined Sinclair in that work, and Mrs. Knight's talents were relegated to *The Beggar's Opera* and *John of Paris*. Possibly her voice had started to deteriorate, for good notices from the papers came less frequently.

The rivalry as well as the differences in productions between the French and English theaters is best seen in their stagings in 1835 of Meyerbeer's *Robert le Diable*. First produced at the Opera in Paris in November 1831, *Robert* was the beginning of the genre of "grand opera" created by Meyerbeer, his librettist Eugène Scribe, and the director of the Opéra, Louis Véron. This, the first of Scribe's librettos for Meyerbeer, had striking scenic effects, a demonic element (shades of *Der Freischütz*), and the sweet heroine and religious overlay that was to appear almost thirty years later in Gounod's *Faust*. The setting was thirteenth-century Italy. *Robert*, a great success and real money-maker for the Paris Opéra, was written for the great French tenor Adolphe Nourrit (a student, incidentally, of Manuel Garcia), the dark-eyed beauty and star soprano Laure Cinti-Damoreau, and conducted by the meticulous François Habeneck, director of concerts at the Paris Conservatory. The colorful orchestration and difficult vocal parts were a challenge for any company. At the American theater Mr. Reynoldson, a bass and new director of music, translated the opera into English, edited the orchestration to comply with the theater orchestra's instruments and capabilities, and served as conductor. The staging on March 30 with Charles Hodges, a member of the stock company, as Robert and Mrs. Knight as Alice was double billed with Oh Hush by Thomas D. "Daddy" Rice, the famous blackface entertainer who originated the character of Jim Crow. Although this was a large, complex work and a major factor in setting the pattern for the French grand opera style in Paris for years to come, in America an afterpiece was considered a necessary part of the bill.

Predictably the French paper caustically criticized the American performance of Robert, while the American press praised it.[43] From such strong partisanship an objective evaluation was hardly possible, but we can observe that Caldwell's company had only fifteen members in the orchestra and was using an actor-singer and a fading soprano for the leads. The French company had an admittedly better orchestra and professional singers and so would have needed fewer alterations in the score. Also, they could use the original language. Although the Orleans Theater production was probably superior, the Camp Street Theater had triumphantly staged it first. Perhaps most important is that two theaters could offer more than a dozen performances of the same work over three months. This strongly attests to New Orleans' reputation as a city of opera lovers.

The city took on the aura of an opera mecca when its enthusiasm expanded to include Italian opera. The year following the productions of Robert, Caldwell brought the Montressor Company and its Italian works to his St. Charles Theater. This is the same Montressor who had collaborated with da Ponte in New York a few years before and had recently gone to Havana. The company, managed by Montressor's son, opened to responsive audiences with Bellini's Il pirata, followed by Norma and Rossini's Otello and Zelmira. Various Italian companies (those of Antonio De Rosa, Francis Brichta, and others whose singers at times shifted companies) would come to New Orleans over the next few years. Many of the French and Italian works were contemporary and introduced only a year or two after their European premieres. This was also true in New York. The number of French, English, and Italian operas heard in New Orleans in the five years after Robert le Diable is extraordinary. The quality rose with the entrance of conductor Eugene Prevost, who had won prizes in composition at the Paris Conservatory, and soprano Julie Calvé. As the final touch it is significant that the Italian works were popular enough to warrant their translation into French by Davis's company.

In 1843 the French company, under new management, was again in New York at Niblo's Garden with Julie Calvé, who made a great hit in *La Fille du régiment*. Two years later the company returned with Calvé and Prevost to open with Rossini's *Guillaume Tell* and continue with Meyerbeer's *Les Huguenots (The Huguenots)* and *Robert le Diable*, Auber's *La Muette de Portici* and a very successful *La Juive (The Jewess)* by Halévy.

John Davis died June 13, 1839, and four years later Caldwell left his theatrical enterprises for other businesses in which he had been involved for some time. He departed for New York at the beginning of the Civil War and died in 1863.

SOUTHERN CIRCUITS

The Seguin company spread English-language operas to a heterogeneous audience in smaller cities in the South as well as the North. Many came, often more than once, to be entertained by the main attraction and whatever accompanied it. In the smaller towns audiences were of necessity not always large, in fact often thin, and at times unruly. This was a golden period for the Seguins who, except for Caldwell's troupe, had the English opera field pretty much to themselves. They traveled extensively and developed a faithful following with their repertory. The routes included Charleston, Augusta, Savannah or Cincinnati, St. Louis, Mobile and others cities over the years. New Orleans, where they opened in January 1842 at the St. Charles Street Theater with their English version of *Norma*, could be counted on for a longer and predictably profitable run. They traveled with two or three additional singers in the troupe and added members from the local stock company to fill out the cast. This practice meant that their performance had to be limited to works the stock company knew or could quickly learn. In late January and the first half of February 1845 the Seguins were in Charleston with a Mr. Frazer, a Mr. Andrews, and Miss Moss in the company to stage *The Bohemian Girl* five times,

La sonnambula, Fra Diavolo, and The Postillion of Longjumeau twice each, and The Dumb Girl of Portici (also called Masaniello) and Amilie; or The Love Test one time each. When the company reached New Orleans on March 3 they retained only the first four works and added Guy Mannering for a total of twelve performances and then proceeded on to Mobile for nine nights.[44] By 1847 when the larger, more glamorous and professional Italian companies appeared as serious competition, the Seguins had become too repetitious, and consequently the repertory turned stale.

DRAMA AND MUSIC

During the 1820s English comic opera lost its exclusive position in the center of the stage and had to make room for translations of contemporary French, Italian, and a few German works. Some common threads have emerged, such as an increasing inclusion of and emphasis on sensational scenes, supernatural powers complete with ghosts, and settings that look back in history. The sensational appeal of the "Wolf's Glen" scene in Der Freischütz found another form that was equally eerie in the ballet of the defrocked nuns who rose from their graves in Robert le Diable to dance wildly around Robert. The Devil (Samiel) of Der Freischütz was a model that reappeared, under Eugène Scribe's pen, as Bertram the devil-father and tempter of the hero in Robert le Diable. Scribe also wrote the libretto for La Dame blanche which calls up a ghost to create its mysterious, gothic atmosphere, but the ghost is more for titillation than sensation, as it turns out to be a person, not a phantom. Likewise, the ghost that appears to terrify the villagers in the modernized pastoral ambience of La sonnambula is substance, in the form of the heroine, rather than shadow. Scribe chose the misty past of the thirteenth century for Robert and used Scott's vividly drawn time of one hundred years earlier for La Dame blanche. No matter what his limitations, Scott offered his readers fascinating historical panoramas that they could learn from and enjoy and offered a rich field for librettists. Fry followed the fashion when he transferred the setting of Leonora back from modern France to sixteenth-century Spain.

As opera texts took on these more "romantic" hues, the musical style of the simpler English songs was exchanged for the Italian bel canto (a type of singing that emphasized a long, smooth melodic line, ornamentation and beautiful tone quality) of Bellini and Donizetti.[45] Bishop's popularity in the second and third decades of the century was widespread, and his songs were sung on many stages. Their plodding repetitions and frequent tonal fixation on one key, no matter how cloying to our ears, apparently were not so to those of his audiences, for his "Home, Sweet Home" was often sung in concert, or inserted into operas by Malibran, Jenny Lind, and Adelina Patti throughout the century. This folk-like tune flourished in a time when distinctions between "popular" and "classical" music did not exist.

Bellini's music was of much higher quality, hardly comparable to Bishop's, but became almost as popular. Donizetti and Bellini's music evolved out of the traditions and style of Rossini but with some alterations, two of which were particularly important. One was the treatment of the vocal line, which in broad terms became simpler and more direct with a lessened possibility for improvisation on the part of the singer. The florid art of the eighteenth-century castrati, which Rossini had grown up with and which had influenced his vocal style, had waned. A second alteration was the development of a more chordal style in which harmonies tended to change at a fairly slow pace. Clearly there were many other changes, too. The many arrangements of songs (arias) from La sonnambula published for amateurs attest to an extraordinary demand, which would only be surpassed in a few years by similar excerpts from Norma.

European opera, accessible in translations, had felt the winds of change that were shifting toward more intense and violent plots with appropriate stylistic developments in the music. The prevalence of comic subjects, or at the least those with a "happy" ending, was on the decline as the new type evolved with its new requirements.

CONCLUSION

In the North, opera was attended by an audience drawn from a limited but expanding population still close culturally to Britain and still using (in its wealthy class) certain rather private symbols of class distinctions.[46] English style opera dominated the period of 1825-1847, with French and Italian works appearing only sporadically in the original language, but often in translation. Performances may have varied in quality and in the actual content of a work, but the use of the English language was considered as essential as the combination of opera with other miscellaneous entertainments to round out the evening. The afterpiece or farce functioned not only to lengthen and add variety to the evening, but also in a manner similar to that of the "lieto fine" (happy ending) of the eighteenth-century opera seria. One left the theater with a pleasant, optimistic feeling. Equally important was the need to please a heterogeneous audience of varied tastes and levels of sophistication, and the afterpiece helped serve that purpose. Before the segregation of opera, drama, comedy, and other genres into special, separate theaters, opera co-existed, democratically, with all other entertainments on one stage. There were no purist objections to following a translated Don Giovanni with an afterpiece. No one was excluded intellectually or financially, for the audience supported opera it could understand and went where the price was uniform. Garcia's staging of Rossini and Mozart masterpieces with their florid arias and sung recitatives was a revelation not only of artistic refinement, but of the genre's potential excitement. John Davis's New Orleans company mounted first-class performances of a fine contemporary French repertory typified by spoken dialogue and shorter solo airs. Maria Garcia Malibran, under the tutelage of her truly gifted father, enchanted her audiences and became the standard by which all female singers were evaluated for several decades. Thus the Garcias, who emphasized Rossini, laid the groundwork for da Ponte's efforts to establish a permanent Italian opera of wider scope. Da Ponte failed just as Palmo would fail, but Italian operatic music became familiar as it was disseminated not only through English language performances but also through band concerts, piano arrangements, and the publications of separate songs in translation.

In New York the wealthy patrons, an essential part of opera from its birth, had been exposed to the enchantment of the Italian and French styles as well as its aristocratic associations by the end of the 1840s. In the next decade Italian opera in particular would attract the attention of the socially elite as they realized that its symbolic significance of exclusivity and prestige could be used as a rung in their own social hierarchy. Concurrently, European performers and managers emerged as advocates of Italian opera in particular. As Philip Hone had noted in 1835, there was at that point no reason for Italian opera to exist in America. The mellifluous marriage of Italian poetry and music had little meaning for or impact on an English-speaking audience, especially because the same lovely melodies with words one could understand were accessible at a theater where prices better reflected egalitarian principles.

A mixed audience went to the opera, or theater that included opera, giving their approval or lack of it with little interference from a critic's opinion, and many returned home to sing and play the music well or badly but with enjoyment. Those opera airs had a pervasive influence on the musical taste of the time.

NOTES

1. Edward Pessen, Riches, Class, and Power before the Civil War (Lexington, MA: D. C. Heath and Co., 1973), Chapter 7.

2. Michael A. Lebowitz, "The Jacksonians: Paradox Lost?," Towards a New Past: Dissenting Essays in American History, ed. Barton J. Bernstein (New York: Random House, 1968), p. 69.

3. David Grimsted, Melodrama Unveiled: American Theater and Culture, 1800-1850 (Chicago: University of Chicago Press, 1968), p 35.

4. Albert Stoutamire, Music of the Old South: Colony to Confederacy (Rutherford, NJ: Fairleigh Dickinson University Press, 1972), pp. 246-247.

5. Julius Mattfeld, *Variety Music Cavalcade: 1620-1950. A Chronology of Vocal and Instrumental Music Popular in the United States* (New York: Prentice-Hall, revised ed. 1962), p. 36.

6. James H. Stone, "Mid-Nineteenth-Century American Beliefs in the Social Values of Music," *Musical Quarterly* XLIII/1 (1957), pp. 38-41.

7. Joseph N. Ireland, *Records of the New York Stage from 1750 to 1860*, 2 vols. (New York: Benjamin Bloom, 1966), vol. 2, p. 295.

8. Richard Montague, "Charles Edward Horn: His Life and Work (1786-1849)" (Ph.D. dissertation, Florida State University, 1959), p. 11. Much of the information on Horn comes from Montague.

9. Rophino Lacy, *Cinderella, or the Fairy Queen and the Little Glass Slipper*, ed. John Graziano (New York: Garland Publishing, Inc., forthcoming 1994). Preface by Professor John Graziano provided the crucial information on *Cinderella*.

10. John Curtis, "One Hundred Years of Grand Opera in Philadelphia" (unpublished typescript at the Historical Society of Pennsylvania in Philadelphia), p. 96.

11. Frederick Corder, "The Works of Sir Henry Bishop," *Musical Quarterly* IV (1918), pp. 78-97.

12. George C. D. Odell, *Annals of the New York Stage* (New York: Columbia University Press, 1927-1937), vol. 3, p. 137.

13. Julius Mattfeld, *A Hundred Years of Grand Opera in New York* (New York: The New York Public Library, 1927) gives repertory and details of the company.

14. Ibid., p. 19.

15. Howard Bushnell, *Maria Malibran: A Biography of the Singer* (University Park, PA: Pennsylvania State University Press, 1979), p. 3.

16. Vera Brodsky Lawrence, *Strong on Music, The New York Music Scene in the Days of George Templeton Strong, 1836-1875*, Vol. I, *Resonances 1836-1850* (New York: Oxford University Press, 1988), p. xl.

17. Mattfeld, *A Hundred Years of Grand Opera in New York*, p. 20.

18. Quoted in Bushnell, *Maria Malibran*, p. 22.

19. Karen Pendle, *Eugène Scribe and French Opera of the Nineteenth Century* (Ann Arbor, MI: UMI Research, 1979), pp. 274-311.

20. Jerome Mitchell, *The Walter Scott Operas* (Birmingham: University of Alabama Press, 1977).

21. Henry Arnold Kmen, *Music in New Orleans: The Formative Years 1791-1841*, pp. 112-113.

22. Ibid., p. 124.

23. Mattfeld, *A Hundred Years of Grand Opera in New York*, p. 19.

24. Sheila Hodges, *Lorenzo Da Ponte: The Life and Times of Mozart's Librettist* (London: Granada Publishing, 1985), pp. 193-194.

25. Quoted in Mattfeld, *A Hundred Years of Grand Opera in New York*, p. 32.

26. William W. Clapp, *A Record of the Boston Stage* (New York: Greenwood Press, reprint 1969), p. 318.

27. Ireland, *Records of the New York Stage*, pp. 71-72.

28. William Treat Upton, *William Henry Fry: American Journalist and Composer-Critic* (New York: Thomas Y. Crowell Company, 1954), pp. 26-27.

29. W. G. Armstrong, *Record of the Opera in Philadelphia* (New York: AMS, 1976), p. 39.

30. David Kimbell, *Italian Opera* (New York: Cambridge University Press, 1991), p. 474.

31. Richard Grant White, "Opera in New York," *The Century* XXIII (1882), p. 701.

32. Lawrence, *Strong on Music*, pp.251-262.

33. Katherine Keenan Preston, "Travelling Opera Troupes in the United States, 1825-1860" (Ph.D. dissertation, City University of New York, 1989), vol. 1, pp. 129, 135.

34. Carl Bode, *The Anatomy of American Popular Culture 1840-1861* (Berkeley: University of California Press, 1960), p. 11.

35. Edwin L. Smith, "William Henry Fry's Leonora" (Ph.D. dissertation, University of Kentucky, 1974), pp. 24, 92, 180.

36. Vera Brodsky Lawrence, "William Henry Fry's Messianic Yearnings: Eleven Lectures, 1852-1853," *American Music* VII/4 (1989): 382-411.

37. White, *Opera in New York*, XXIV, p. 202.

38. Max Maretzek, *Revelations of an Opera Manager in Nineteenth-Century America. Crotchets and Quavers, Sharps and Flats.* (New York: Dover, 1968), p. 20.

39. H. Earle Johnson, *Musical Interludes in Boston 1795-1830* (New York: Columbia University Press, 1943), pp. 39-46, 61.

40. Nelle Smither, *A History of the English Theatre at New Orleans 1806-1842* (New York: Benjamin Blom, Inc., reissued 1967), p. 49.

41. Ibid., p. 52.

42. John S. Kendall, *The Golden Age of the New Orleans Theater* (Baton Rouge: Louisiana State University Press, 1952), p. 37.

43. Kmen, *Music in New Orleans*, pp.135-137.

44. Preston, "Travelling Opera Troupes," pp. 480, 485. Stoutamire, Music of the Old South, p. 185.

45. The New Harvard Dictionary of Music, ed. Don Michael Randel (Cambridge, MA: The Belknap Press of Harvard University Press, 1986).

46. Pessen, Riches, Class, and Power, Chapter 11.

4

European Versus English Style: 1847–1865

From out of ancient fairy tales
There beckons a white hand,
There's a singing and a ringing
Of an enchanted land;
Heinrich Heine
in Robert Schumann's Dichterliebe

Italian musical style and American romantic-wilderness myth coalesced in the opera, La Spia by Luigi Arditi (1822-1905). The Italian composer and conductor based his libretto on James Fenimore Cooper's best selling novel The Spy, a colorful thriller set in the days of the Revolution. Arditi, a first rate musician and violinist, created a well-crafted Italian style opera that received a positive, if conservative, reaction from the journal The Albion. While the critic, interestingly enough, lauded La Spia's predictability and lack of originality, he did protest at the interjection of "Hail, Columbia" in Act III.[1] The opera was repeated five times in March of 1856 at New York's Academy of Music under Arditi's direction with a cast that included European soprano Anna de La Grange, tenor Pasquale Brignoli at the beginning of a highly successful American career and twenty-year-old Elise Hensler, the daughter of a Boston tailor. Shortly after her performances, Miss Hensler sailed for Europe to continue her career at the Royal Opera House in Lisbon. Prince Ferdinand of Portugal, the former king-consort, saw her performance one night and rapidly fell in love with the talented and beautiful young

American. He arranged to meet her, declared his feelings, and ardently pressed his suit. Miss Hensler was charmed and flattered, but like a good Boston girl, firmly refused any proposal short of marriage. The Prince therefore had to negotiate the difficult problems of bringing a commoner, and a foreigner at that, into the royal family. He succeeded, of course, and eventually they were married, at which time she left the musical stage to live out her life in castles in Portugal. Life had imitated operatic drama and fantasy as this Cinderella-like story of the daughter of a Boston tailor unfolded.[2] Anything was possible, as the magical world of opera repeatedly proposed to audiences.

THE BACKDROP

By the late 1840s faith in the efficacy of education, a sense of mission that was part of the legacy of the Jacksonian era, and a firm belief in progress were "givens" for many Americans. The "educational awakening" of the 1830s with its expanded use of libraries and museums was alive and well and managed to maintain its momentum up to the Civil War. Beneath this optimism and belief in progress, however, the issue of slavery with its immorality, horrors, injustice and as a political controversy festered to absorb increasing attention, time, and energy.

Religion was dominated by the Protestant Church with a widening evangelical streak. Church leaders spoke out on the problems of slavery and other social issues, articulating the humanitarian sentiments of members of the congregation and many outside. As de Tocqueville had noted in his Democracy in America, "religion is mingled with all the national customs and all those feelings which the word fatherland evokes. For that reason it has peculiar power."[3] It would continue to play a major role in people's lives as it balanced spiritual values against competitive, materialistic drives. Missionaries followed pioneers to the West to build congregations and attempted to convert the Indians. A sense of "mission" drove the reform movements in which antislavery sentiments often figured. Another facet of this idealistic concern with social problems appeared in the many utopian community experiments of the first half of the century. Although one of the best known, Brook Farm, was finally dissolved, other visionary groups, of all stripes, continued to spring up.

European political strife of the 1840s and 1850s, coupled with sporadic failure of crops, brought waves of immigrants, including musicians, to our shores. Germans in particular, retreating from the revolutions of 1848 and ensuing social disorder as old regimes collapsed, emigrated to America to enrich our musical life as they created choral groups, added to orchestras, and enlarged audiences. By mid-century the economy was expanding with an inflow of foreign money, growth of railroads and the subsequent development of business. As population and wealth grew, possibilities for leisure entertainment, music, and theater increased. The discovery of gold in California added to a sense of optimism, well-being, and prosperity that flowed on, marred only by a minor recession in 1857-1858, to the Civil War.

With the exception of opera houses, theaters, as Harper's Weekly (I, 1857) noted, continued to attract a riotous element that gambled, drank, encouraged prostitution, and ruined the surrounding neighborhood. Northern and Southern theaters maintained designated sections for single women (i.e., prostitutes), and leased concessions for bars to maximize profits. The clergy had reason to complain and continued to attack the stage, but with less attention to and impact on that more respectable genre, the opera.

Several major factors that had long-range implications for opera emerged by mid-century. First, as opera companies proliferated, their structure and repertory changed. Stock companies more and more frequently left opera to professional singers and managers who now came less often from Britain than from the Continent, bringing with them contemporary Italian works. As these companies became firmly entrenched in the 1850s, they began to displace the English operas and translations, which had started to suffer from overexposure anyway and consequently were losing some of their attraction. Even British companies with well-trained singers found the competition stiff. Moreover, the old arrangements, such as those by Charles Horn, which actors could sing, seemed simple and naive compared to the sophisticated, professional performances of the Italian singers who had the advantage of growing up and training in the operatic hothouse of Italy. The vocal accomplishments and glamour of performers such as Fortunata Tedesco, Natale Perelli, and later Marietta Alboni and Angolina Bosio combined to create a more magical world of fantasy and move the genre into a more rarefied sphere of theater. Although Italian language opera rapidly gained a foothold, English opera persisted as a variety of troupes toured Eastern cities and took advantage of the rapidly expanding railroad system to seek new audiences.

Second, a company's central figure now was often a manager who, unlike the past, was not an actor or singer in the troupe, but a person who handled the expanding business activities of the company. He hired, fired, advertised, negotiated, and objectively assessed the audience potential as he determined what would be most profitable financially. This manager probably conducted or, more accurately, directed the performances. This still could mean leading the orchestra from the first violin position or from the piano. Conducting as we now know it came about only slowly and sporadically.[4]

Third, more and more often attempts were made to identify opera companies solely with an opera house, thus separating the genre from other types of entertainment. Even though its uses might be diverse, the opera house began to have a clear identification that attracted and was supported by a growing, wealthy social class that further projected an image of exclusivity. A foreign language repertory, imported foreign stars, and higher priced tickets served to sharpen that image as the wealthy turned to opera and the opera house as a place to meet others of a similar social and economic group: their crowd. This was similar to the opera house in Italy, which until mid-century functioned as a sort of civic center in which all sorts of social and business transactions took place.

Underneath these changes lay another important factor: the Janus face of the American's attitude toward the arts. On one side there is the chauvinistic smile that proudly approves of all things "American" and on the other a begrudging admiration for European culture and art and a secret belief in its superiority. These attitudes were reflected in writings about music that appeared by mid-century in newspapers and journals in cities where well-informed, able writers were employed.[5] American artists and their creations were seen as inferior to any European work; regarding music, this attitude unfortunately survives to this day in many circles.

THE HAVANA COMPANY

The Havana Opera Company presented excellent performances of a contemporary Italian repertory, in Italian, in New York in the spring of 1847.[6] With its superior singers and ensemble and excellent director, Luigi Arditi, the company opened at the Park in the American premiere of Verdi's Ernani. The Havana's manager, Don Francisco Marti y Torrens, had built the impressive Tacon Theater in Havana and supported the company with his considerable wealth gained by his strong-arm control and monopoly of the Cuban fish market.[7] Although Marty, who was reputed to have started out as a pirate, knew little about music, he recognized opera's social status value and hoped that his opera house would open the doors of Cuban society for him. To this end he employed effective agents to hire the best singers and instrumentalists available. Despite his excellent company, Cuba's aristocracy ignored it and him, but rather than sit in his theater as the sole member of the audience, he sent the company on periodic tours primarily to keep it together and also to get it out of Cuba during the "sick season" when malaria or yellow fever became a scourge. A few weeks after their acclaimed New York opening, the troupe, according to critics, electrified the more staid Boston audiences with the singing of its stars Fortunata Tedesco and Natale Perelli. The statuesque Tedesco's voice was described as "rich, voluptuous" and her duets with Perelli described as "exquisitely" beautiful, although the acting was considered generally unimpressive.[8] Besides fine principal singers, the chorus and orchestra were large and Arditi's conducting authoritative.

Repertory, in addition to Verdi's Ernani, I due Foscari (The Two Foscari), and I Lombardi, included Pacini's Saffo and later the familiar Norma. Despite the prevalence of Verdi's works, they initially received a mixed reception and were compared unfavorably, by some critics, to the older style of Bellini and Donizetti. American critics were not alone, for similar protests had been raised in Italy and elsewhere.[9] Verdi's more frequent scoring for brass and percussion was perceived as noisy, overly complex, and generally lacking beauty. Nevertheless, the Italian company's performances so impressed Boston audiences and critics that the English opera repertory seemed pale by comparison, slowly lost the ability to generate enthusiasm, and never really regained its stature. In Philadelphia the Havana Company's excellent singers and conductor were also extolled.[10] For the next five years the "Havana Company," with fluctuating personnel although the same name, gave seasons in larger cities from New York to New Orleans with great success.

English language opera, however, died in true operatic fashion, that is, very slowly. Shortly after the Havana's triumphs Anna Bishop, second wife of the famous English opera composer Henry Bishop, staged an English version of Donizetti's Linda di Chamounix in New York. Mrs. Bishop had left her husband and children a number of years earlier for a harpist named Charles Bochsa (the "Paganini of the harp") with whom she toured Europe in concerts.[11] An attractive, elegant lady who understood the intricacies of public relations quite well, she held soirées for local critics and other key figures before her debut here. Mrs. Bishop's lovely voice, fine technique, and extensive wardrobe of fashionable costumes assured her an enthusiastic reception by audiences everywhere she went with only a few dissenting voices.[12] Other works in which Mrs. Bishop starred included the premiere of Michael Balfe's Maid of Artois, written for Maria Malibran, and the English version of Bellini's La sonnambula. Selected scenes from a variety of operas that showed her vocal and histrionic abilities to best advantage supplemented her repertory.

One writer critical of Mrs. Bishop was Richard Grant White, (1821-1885), a graduate of Columbia College who had studied medicine and law but turned to journalism and scholarly pursuits. He was critic for music, art, and literature on the Morning Courier and New York Enquirer until 1859, also wrote editorials and articles on politics and contributed to such journals as North

American Review, Atlantic Monthly, and the London Spectator. White became a noted scholar of Shakespeare, published many articles on the bard and his works and edited twelve volumes of his plays. An exacting critic, he was at times severe, but held to clear, high musical standards.

ASTOR PLACE OPERA HOUSE

Italian opera as a symbol of wealth and social position emerged most concretely in late 1847 with the construction of the Astor Place Opera House on Eighth Street between Broadway and Lafayette Street. A group of wealthy men induced about 150 affluent, socially inclined subscribers to support financially the venture, for which, in return, the subscriber would receive a set number of admissions. A few years later opera in general was described by journalist and critic N. P. Willis as:

> the one fashionable amusement which has been selected as a center for a Dress Exchange--a substitute for a general drawing room--a refined attraction which the ill-mannered would not be likely to frequent, and around which the higher classes might gather, for the easier interchange of courtesies, and for that closer view which aides the candidacy or acquaintance.[13]

At the Astor Place Opera House the dress code of white kid gloves required for gentlemen would, and did, put off and infuriate many, while the foreign language repertory, with its snobbish implications, could almost be guaranteed to bore, discourage or intimidate the uninitiated. The opera house opened in November of 1847 with Verdi's Ernani under the management of singers Sanquirico and Patti, who had performed earlier that year at the ill-fated Palmo's. Similarly, Astor Place followed a persistent pattern of financial failure when managers concentrated on Italian opera alone with its smaller audience. William Niblo, and then Edward P. Fry, brother of the composer of Leonora, followed Sanquirico and Patti as managers with similar financial deficits. Max Maretzek, however, as conductor and impresario managed to achieve slightly more profitable seasons. He became, in the spring of 1849 "the 'successful candidate for the lease and direction of the said establishment' [Astor Place Opera House]" the day following a bloody riot at Astor Place that resulted in as many as thirty-four dead and fifty injured.[14]

The riot, to outward appearances, was caused by the twenty-year-old simmering feud between two celebrated actors, the aristocratic Englishman William Macready and the volatile, somewhat suspicious American, Edwin Forrest. Underlying the riot was the animosity directed at the Opera House as an anti-democratic, elitist symbol complete with a dress code and foreign language proclivity. Macready was performing in Macbeth at the Astor Place Opera House as the conclusion of an American tour when Forrest provocatively announced that he too would enact Macbeth in another theater on the same night. Forrest supporters in the Astor Place audience pelted Macready with various objects at his first appearance, and rowdiness turned into a tumultuous riot. On the following evening police and soldiers were sent into the area to prevent continued mob violence and damage, but the unrest continued for three nights. The socially fashionable opera house as a proponent of "high" culture had established a beachhead and met those of "low" culture head on, and for a brief time the theater was rechristened the "Massacre" Opera House.[15] Shortly it would have a new manager and, although soon it would lose its prestige to descend to the level of performing dogs and monkeys, the determination of Italian opera supporters to have a special theater for the "in group" had been made crystal clear.

The new manager, Maximilian Maretzek (1821-1897), a sophisticated, experienced musician with extensive musical contacts, would shortly become a major figure in opera in America. Born in Moravia, Czechoslovakia, "Maretzek the Magnificent," as Clara Louise Kellogg says he was always called,[16] had known Meyerbeer, Berlioz, Chopin and Liszt in Paris, worked at Covent Garden in London and from there been hired by Edward Fry as conductor and music director at Astor Place. In November of 1849 this handsome, charismatic conductor opened a season of opera with Donizetti's Lucia di Lammermoor, Don Pasquale, and the American premiere of Maria di Rohan followed by Rossini's

Barber of Seville, Otello, and Verdi's Ernani. Ever alert for talent, Maretzek heard the highly-touted Havana Opera Company at Castle Garden in New York that summer of 1850 and was so impressed that he hired as many of the musicians as possible for his own troupe. Among them was his future wife, Apollonia Bertucca, a bewitching Rosina in Barber, a talented singer and harpist who accompanied herself on that instrument in Desdemona's "Willow Song" in Rossini's Otello.

THE NORTHEAST

Maretzek noted that there were three equally important musical centers in the Northeast--Philadelphia, New York, and Boston--that he used alternatively for his various companies and tours.[17] Among the many singers he introduced to American audiences during the early 1850s, two who stood out were Teresa Parodi and Teresa Truffi. The latter was perceived as handsome with a very dramatic style; her powerful mezzo was compelling, but marred by a tremolo.[18] Parodi, supposedly the favorite pupil of world renowned soprano Giuditta Pasta, had been given extensive advance publicity in the hope of countering the public's current love affair with Jenny Lind. Starred in Donizetti's popular Lucrezia Borgia, she was later described by Dwight as a bold and muscular Lucrezia.[19]

Music critic John Sullivan Dwight (1813-1893) created this country's first truly fine periodical devoted solely to music, Dwight's Journal of Music, which he published from 1852-1881. A graduate of Harvard Divinity School who spent a brief period as a Unitarian minister, Dwight joined Brook Farm's group of intellectuals to teach Latin and music, work on the farm, and soon to write and edit the group's periodical, The Harbinger. When he left at the demise of this utopian enterprise, he turned to music, his other great passion besides social reform, and started his own weekly music periodical, aiming, as he stated in the first issue, to be "impartial, independent, catholic, conciliatory; aloof from personal cliques and feuds." The Journal had many important contributors (e.g., Alexander Wheelock Thayer, the biographer of

Beethoven, Lowell Mason, the foremost music educator of his day, and others) who brought informed and enlightening information to its readers. It provides us today with an invaluable first-hand view of these musical times and performers. Among the latter, Dwight gave unstinting praise to Jenny Lind by the time of her farewell concert in May 1852.

Although the soprano did not perform in operas in this country, she had just retired (1850) from a highly successful European operatic career, and arias were staple items in her American concerts. Those concert programs reflected the current popularity of Italian opera as well as continuing to popularize it. In fact, opera excerpts, vocal and instrumental, were standard fare on musical programs of all types throughout the nineteenth century. Overtures appeared regularly in band concerts while "fantasies" for piano, consisting of transcribed arias or a melange of "highlights," were composed by everyone from Liszt to Gottschalk. The dissemination of operatic music was probably equaled only by that of "popular" songs.

P. T. Barnum, Lind's shrewd manager, chose Castle Garden for her well planned American debut. His public relation tactics included well-timed newspaper items about his "Swedish Nightingale," which generated large crowds on her arrival and an auction of the tickets to her first concert, an idea used many times thereafter. The program, in two parts, consisted of Lind's rendition of "Casta Diva" from Norma, a trio for voice and flutes from a Meyerbeer opera written for her (Ein Feldlager in Schlesien, or A Camp in Silesia), and her specialty, the "Echo Song," as well as two duets from Rossini operas with baritone Giovanni Belletti, an aria from Rossini's Barber sung by Belletti, a two-piano piece by famous pianist Thalberg and two opera overtures.[20] Conductor Julius Benedict wrote the closing "Greeting to America" especially for the occasion. Later that month her programs would include popular arias from Bellini's I puritani and La sonnambula, Meyerbeer's Robert le Diable and Mozart's Magic Flute. Frequently she added such favorites as "Home, Sweet Home," which became her trademark, or the "Last Rose of Summer" to her opera selections. Despite the enthusiasm of audiences (and Dwight), many reservations as to the quality of Lind's voice were noted, such as those put forth by a writer for The Albion:

> why with so many excellences, and such great instructors, she has still so many faults. She has had, we believe, much to contend against; her voice naturally was, undoubtedly, an impracticable organ. . . . Naturally it is not flexible; . . . The difficulty between the registers is distinctly seen.[21]

The public, however, adored her, and her generosity to charities, well advertised by Barnum, considerably enhanced her positive image.

In 1854 a new opera house that would become a New York landmark, the Academy of Music, was inaugurated under manager Maretzek with a performance of Norma by two of the most glittering European stars of the day, Giulia Grisi and Giovanni Mario. The Academy, which was supported by some of the same stockholders that had financed the Astor Place Opera House, would remain unchallenged as a home for opera until the construction of the Metropolitan Opera in 1883. The term "academy" implied an educational purpose that was never really explored, but signified an awareness of the need to train home grown talent rather than relying so heavily on expensive, imported performers such as Grisi and Mario. Another theater of a less formal sort that served opera well in the early 1850s was the open air theater in Niblo's Garden. Operas in English as well as other entertainments had been staged at moderate prices in the attractive surroundings of the Garden by excellent singers for more than a decade, for large, heterogeneous audiences. By 1853 Henrietta Sontag and Marietta Alboni, both distinguished artists, sang Italian works there, attracting, even at higher prices, large audiences and considerable critical acclaim. Like New York, Philadelphia built an Academy, which was inaugurated with Il trovatore (The Troubadour) in 1857, but again any educational purpose soon disappeared.

Il trovatore, like Norma, was one of the most popular operas in nineteenth-century America. First performed in Rome in 1853 Verdi's complex, dark tale of vengeance based on a highly successful drama by a prominent, Spanish playwright Gutiérrez, reached New York two years later. Composed during Italy's struggle for unification, when the opera house in Italy was a social, business, and recreational center, Il trovatore, similar to other Verdi works, took on political implications for its audiences. By then the strongly nationalistic Verdi had became a symbol for political unification and audiences repeatedly saw in his librettos parallels to their own conflicted time.

The composer painted the opera's fifteenth-century Spanish setting in somber, almost sinister colors, as he unfolded a complex plot that bombards the audience with dramatic and even violent events in quick succession. While this is not strictly a horror story, it contains elements of horror in a plot as convoluted as the music is inspired. At the center of the libretto are the two main female roles of Leonora and the gypsy Azucena and their individual relationships to Manrico, the solitary, romantic troubadour who sings love songs, champions freedom, and is executed at the end. For the heroine, Leonora, whose intense conflict between love and sin is only resolved by taking poison, Verdi wrote one of his most brilliant roles. In Azucena, the tormented gypsy whose mother was burned at the stake, who will herself meet the same fate, and who has inadvertently killed her own child, the composer created one of his most fully-rounded operatic roles. These characters in Il trovatore generally lack self-doubt and have an unclouded moral confidence that duty either to God or country, or both, is more important than personal happiness.

BRISTOW

In spite of the growing presence of Italian opera at mid-century, an opera on an American subject by an American composer was successfully staged at Niblo's theater in September 1855: Rip Van Winkle by George Frederick Bristow (1825-1898). It has been suggested that the composer may have been responding to the $1,000 prize offered by Ole Bull for an American opera, and this may indeed have been the case.[22] Bristow was well known to the musical community of New York as a violinist with the Philharmonic Society and as conductor of the extensive musical examples with orchestra and singers for William Henry Fry's highly publicized lectures of 1852-1853.[23] In the following year

Bristow publicly (if briefly) resigned from the Philharmonic because of what he termed an "anti-American" attitude toward performing American works. His point was well taken, and he established himself, along with Fry, as a strong supporter of American music and as an advocate for the American composer. Besides being a capable violinist and solid conductor, this modest man who spent considerable energy teaching in New York's public schools, also held prestigious church jobs as organist-choir director, was a good clarinetist, a fine pianist, and wrote a fair amount of music.

He conducted the Pyne and Harrison English Opera Company in the premiere of his only completed opera, Rip Van Winkle. The company had been performing at Niblo's since May in a long successful season that would include seventeen performances (a very large number for the time) of Bristow's opera. One of the reviews noted events in the Crimean War as comparable to those taking place on the musical stage:

> Sebastopol has fallen, and a new American Opera has succeeded in New York! The clash of Russian steel with the bristling bayonets of the Allies has not been more fierce and uncompromising than the strife in lyric art between the strong hold of foreign prejudice, and the steady and combined attacks of native musicians.[24]

Reviews were generally positive to mixed regarding the work and performance. The Pyne and Harrison company, unfortunately, did not take on the opera as part of their standard repertory for subsequent tours. As with Fry's Leonora, the large cast was a hindrance as probably was the music, which was rather extensive and complex for a supporting stock company to learn quickly.

Bristow's librettist, J. H. Wainwright, based his plot on Washington Irving's famous Rip Van Winkle, which was published in 1819 and later appeared as a popular play. Act I presents Rip, who likes his liquor a bit too much, squabbling with his critical wife in their village in the "Kaatskills" in 1763. The argument terminates as Rip leaves home to fall asleep in the mountains where he is visited by various spirits. Act II (during Rip's long slumber) reveals his aging wife, their daughter (Alice) and son

(Rip, Jr.) and Alice's romantic problems with two suitors of opposing political persuasions, her inheritance, and a secret marriage contract. In Act III Rip awakens, returns to his village to discover twenty years have passed, his wife is dead, and the world has changed and is now post-Revolution. He is reunited with his children and manages to solve his daughter's romantic dilemma. The libretto's weakness lies in its rather diffuse style and lack of dramatic tension and shape. Since music tends to slow action anyway, the problem becomes accentuated in an operatic setting. Several critics at the time ventured that the libretto could be advantageously shortened.[25]

Generally, Bristow's harmonic style and formal structures are typical of the earlier nineteenth century. Although there is spoken dialogue, much of the action is carried on in sung recitative, placing this work somewhere between English and Italian opera. The music ranges from the folk-like swing of Rip's drinking song in the first act, "The Gentry may talk," to the strong hymn-like choral opening of Act II, or pieces with a lyrical, more dramatic quality. Edward's aria in Act II reflects an Italian bel canto sense of line and flow but without the usual extension or development. Generally, orchestral writing seems stronger than vocal, for in the latter musical ideas often become repetitious. Another performance took place in Philadelphia in 1870 in a version subsequently published by G. Schirmer in 1882, but the work never entered the mainstream repertory.[26]

POPULARITY AND FAMILIARITY

The popularity of operas can be measured not only by the number and frequency of performances, but also by the quantity of sheet music publications and the number of travesties or versions that appear. Bellini's Norma is a case in point.

One of the most frequently staged works in the decades before and immediately following the Civil War, Norma had been premiered in Milan in 1831 and was staged in Philadelphia under Fry in 1840. The English text was by Fry's brother, Joseph, and William himself worked on setting the music to the new words with as few changes as possible. As was customary, selections were published as sheet music shortly after the performance so that the public could take their favorite pieces home to sing, play, and enjoy. "Casta Diva," Jenny Lind's choice for her opening concert in New York, became "Chaste Goddess." Besides the initial Philadelphia publications, eight vocal excerpts were published in Boston in 1839 in the version that became the best known. In addition, popular songs used tunes from Norma with new words, simplified versions appeared in instruction books for singers and instrumentalists, and piano and band arrangements appeared. Thus the student or amateur musician could become well acquainted with the music, and the libretto was also available.[27]

On a less serious note, Norma eventually became a travesty called Mis-Normer, "in which the Druidic priestess was transformed into a New Orleans' coffee vendor and the Britons and Romans became rival market gangs." The text is cleverly transformed as:

Norma:
Shine forth, young moon,
beneath thy light
Norma will sacrifice
tonight.

Mis-Normer:
Shine forth, young sharks,
although you're tight
Normer's coffee'll set you
right.[28]

There was also a version called Mrs. Normer, but whether it was the same as Mis-Normer is uncertain.[29]

RISE OF THE MANAGERS

Around mid-century, a time when opera "flourished on failure," a shift in the personnel of troupes occurred as the leading singer heading the company ceded increasingly involved management to an impresario who might also conduct.[30] This manager had not only to attend to the leasing of the theater and other financial arrangements, as well as pre-opera publicity, printing of programs, tickets, and such, but also to the delicate problems of placating jealous prima donnas and maneuvering through the byzantine intrigues of the Italian stars who were hired by trips to Europe or by agents there. The most influential of these impresarios were Max Maretzek, Maurice Strakosch, and Bernard Ullmann.

Maretzek had studied composition with Ignaz von Seyfried, (a noted composer and student of Haydn), moved in the elite Parisian and London musical circles noted above and composed two operas, ballet music, and some miscellaneous pieces. For several years prior to his engagement as conductor at the Astor Place Opera House, he had been choral director and assistant conductor at Covent Garden under composer Michael Balfe. When this sophisticated, skillful entrepreneur first heard Marti's Havana troupe he recognized its excellence, saw that it made a sensation in New York and not only hired singers, but also the conductor and virtuoso violinist Luigi Arditi and the renowned double bassist Giovanni Bottesini. Despite the fine company which consisted of sopranos Steffanone, Bertucca, and Bosio, contralto Vietti, tenors Salvi, Bettini, and Lorini, baritones Badiali and Corradi Setti, and basses Marini and Coletti, Maretzek's three month season at Castle Garden ended in debt rather than profit. Through fat and lean years this influential impresario promoted Italian opera in East Coast cities and beyond until the opening of the Metropolitan Opera House in 1883.

Maretzek's occasional partner, Bernard Ullmann, was characterized by a strong instinct for public relations.[31] He claimed to have studied with Beethoven's student Carl Czerny and certainly understood not only how to develop interest in a performer but also how to handle the artist cleverly for the most profit. He attracted large audiences by his public relations and ensured the success of a repeat performance by managing to find some new angle for it. One of his most celebrated singers was the beautiful and gracious Henrietta Sontag, who had married into the aristocracy but fallen on hard times financially and hence decided to return to the stage. Working on the personal interest value of his singer, who also was truly gifted, Ullmann published two books about her before she opened in New York at Niblo's Garden in 1853. The Times then happily reported her voice as "remarkable, even among soprano voices, for its equality of volume and tone . . . it has but one quality of sound; as a violin would have, if all its notes came on one string."[32] Although a poor administrator, according to Maretzek, Ullmann possessed a crucial sense of timing of unfailing value to those he represented. That summer Ullmann joined with Maretzek to present the great contralto, Marietta Alboni, whose sumptuous voice so impressed Walt Whitman, at Castle Garden. Richard Grant White declared her the greatest singer since Malibran and rhapsodized about her voice "It has a lusciousness which is peculiar. It comes bubbling, gurgling, gushing from that full throat and those gently parted lips and reminds of draughts of which poets have sung, but of which Bacchantes have only dreamed."[33]

Maretzek and Maurice Strakosch (1825-1887), both from Moravia, had come to the United States in 1848 and joined in Edward Fry's Grand Musical Festival in October of that year with Maretzek as conductor and Strakosch as pianist. The latter had made his concert debut in Germany as a pianist at age eleven and also studied singing. Shortly after he came to this country he married Amalia Patti, daughter of singer Salvatore Patti and sister of Adelina, who later achieved extraordinary international fame. Strakosch was one of her teachers and took her on a concert tour when she was seven. A keen judge of talent, he also brought tenor Brignoli and baritone Amodio from Europe for the first American performances of Il trovatore in which the former sang Manrico and the latter the Count di Luna. Strakosch joined forces with Ullmann "until then a confirmed enemy" in 1853 to lease the Academy of Music in New York.[34] Apparently willing to stretch his imagination to tickle his public's curiosity, and probably following Ullmann's lead, Strakosch fancifully claimed that one of his star tenors named Tiberini was actually descended directly from the Roman Emperor Tiberius. Equally fanciful was his description of Marietta Piccolomini's lineage as descending from Max Piccolomini, the hero of Schiller's Wallenstein, and stretching back to Charlemagne. Piccolomini's most lasting claim to fame may be that Arditi wrote his famous "Il bacio" ("The Kiss") for her, and it lasted on programs well into this century to be sung by stars such as Joan Sutherland.

Strakosch's more practical business sense, coupled with Ullmann's innovative public relations tactics, worked pretty well. Their partnership managed to survive at the Academy for three years despite their consistent financial losses. These were mainly due to the practice of giving the stockholders the front boxes at no cost and filling unsold seats with "deadheads" (free tickets). The managers could not recoup their losses by the usual tours to Philadelphia and Boston, because their wily rival Maretzek had leased the Academy of Music in Philadelphia for his Havana Company and for several seasons opened just before them in Boston to win the audience's first flush of enthusiasm. Eventually Ullmann and Strakosch solved the Boston situation by making the Boston Theater, also now renamed the Academy, a part of their circuit. During a period of financial stress they turned to a talented unknown who literally saved their season: sixteen-year-old Adelina Patti. She debuted in November 1859 in Lucia di Lammermoor. As her reputation rapidly grew, several, including Strakosch, claimed they had coached her in the role, but it seems most likely that the task had been undertaken by Emanuele Muzio, an associate of Verdi.

Adelina Patti came from an unusually talented family. Besides her opera singing parents (her mother was singing Norma several hours prior to Adelina's birth), her sisters Clotilde, Carlotta, and Amalia were all successful singers. The latter's marriage to Maurice Strakosch formed an important managerial alliance for the family. Her brother Carlo studied violin with Arditi and became conductor at the New Orleans Opera House and later in New York and St. Louis.[35] At her debut Adelina sang with Pasquale Brignoli, who became one of the most celebrated tenors of his time, if, as noted by Boston critic William Apthorp, a terrible actor.[36] Patti left the country shortly before the Civil War for Europe; we will return to her later when she herself returned to America.

Lucia, which became a familiar and popular work with audiences everywhere, was successfully premiered in Naples in

1835 and was given in Paris with Anne Thillon in the somewhat abbreviated French version that came to New Orleans two years later. Soon the Havana Company staged the Italian version, and by 1843 it was in New York. The critic of Spirit of the Times positively glowed over the performance at Palmo's Opera House in March 1844 as he reported that "In the mad scenes she [Eufrasia Borghese] was indeed great . . . in the spirit, the inspiration, even, with which she rendered the glorious music of her part . . . . It was, indeed, her greatest triumph."[37]

Lucia's popularity emanated from several of its dramatic and musical facets. Based on the enormously popular Scott novel The Bride of Lammermoor, it was set at the end of the sixteenth century and offered as thick a brew of ghosts, castles, the past, madness and love betrayed as Scott ever created. Librettist Salvatore Cammarano, who also wrote Verdi's Il trovatore, retained the characters and main events of the novel but focused the conflict on the two feuding families, betrayal, and a thwarted love that results in murder and madness. Emphasis is on the exciting aspects of the plot, which unfolds with its strong, honest hero, a faithful, if passive, misunderstood and long-suffering heroine, fast action and clearly motivated characters. Throughout, Cammarano highlighted a number of evocative, "romantic" references. A particularly effective one occurs at the beginning when Lucia relates that she has seen the ghost of a woman stabbed by her sweetheart beside the fountain in the garden and thus foretells her own fateful story. As the aristocratic Scottish family in its castle destroys itself through autocratic behavior and greed, an implicit message of the evils of a monarchy and its attendant system is conveyed. Audiences saw this intensely romantic drama, whose details they knew well from the novel, illuminated anew by Donizetti's wonderful music. The opera figures in two monumental nineteenth-century novels, Flaubert's Madame Bovary and Tolstoy's Anna Karenina, attesting to its resonance with its times.

The composer wrote the role of Lucia, as well as several others, for Fanny Tacchinardi-Persiani. In developing the character he was influenced by the singer's style, taking advantage of her wide range, extraordinary vocal flexibility, and ability to project high musical intensity. This wonderfully virtuosic soprano role has attracted great prima donnas ever since, from Adelina Patti to Joan Sutherland. The composer set his text with appealingly beautiful, liquid, melodic lines over clear, uncomplicated accompaniments. Harmony and orchestration become richer with all their suggestive powers according to shifts of the dramatic tension through long scenes or acts. Donizetti's mastery of the dramatic moment or his ability to create an arresting, memorable melodic gesture are striking. Although some of his and Bellini's works (such as Lucia and Norma) have rarely been out of the repertory, their style was drowned out in the Wagnerian and verismo waves of the latter part of the century. Only recently have they and their compatriot Rossini received serious attention, as musicologists have undertaken complete editions of their works. Finally they have begun to win a much-needed reassessment.

A TRAVELING COMPANY

Luigi Arditi refers briefly in his Reminiscences to a tour in 1853 in which he would share the role of impresario with soprano Rosa Devries.[38] If impresarios became a major influence on opera at mid-century, so did Arditi as a conductor. Born in 1822 in a small Italian town, Arditi went to the Milan Conservatory to study violin and composition and spent two years conducting in one of the smaller Milan theaters. At twenty-four he was recruited by Badiali, the agent for the wealthy Cuban entrepreneur Marti and brother of a famous baritone, Cesare Badiali, then singing with the Havana Opera Company. Composer of a relatively small body of work, including three operas, Arditi made a concert tour in 1848, between engagements as conductor with Marti's company, with the double bass virtuoso Bottesini, a friend from student days. The tour of 1853 with Devries, who later became an important star of the Paris Opéra, offers a prototype of certain aspects of contemporary tours, such as the prevailing repertory, the time required for travel and performance, and the typical cities that a company could profitably visit.

The company's repertory consisted of the following:

Bellini's Norma and La sonnambula; Donizetti's Belisario, L'elisir d'amore (The Elixir of Love), La favorita (The Favorite), La figlia del reggimento, Lucia di Lammermoor, Lucrezia Borgia; Mozart's Don Giovanni; Rossini's Il barbiere di Siviglia; and Verdi's Ernani. Rossini's Stabat Mater, obviously not an opera, was included because it was an immensely popular work and could be given in concerts that were scheduled in addition to the opera performances. An advantage of this repertory, as opposed to that of a later time, was the consistency of language and musical styles. Only the Rossini and Mozart works required earlier techniques.

The tour opened June 20, 1853, with Lucia di Lammermoor and lasted until August 18, 1854, when it closed with Norma. Performances were staged in Montreal, Toronto, Buffalo, Cincinnati, Louisville, St. Louis, Chicago, Milwaukee, Detroit, Pittsburgh, Baltimore, Washington, D.C., Richmond, Charleston, Savannah, Augusta, Mobile, New Orleans, Memphis, Nashville, Cleveland and Rochester. The longest single residence was, predictably, in New Orleans with nineteen performances, while smaller cities had as few as two or three. The company traveled by railroad and river, and if cities such as St. Louis, Cincinnati and those in the East had already heard English as well as some French and even Italian companies, others such as Chicago and Detroit were fairly new territory. The casts sang sometimes for two or three consecutive nights, but more usually every second or third night with a hiatus of a week here or there, probably because of travel arrangements.[39]

This daunting undertaking involved a cast of about a dozen principal singers, a chorus, and orchestra and exemplifies the energy and sheer determination of managers Arditi and Devries as they presented their contemporary Italian repertory. An important factor in drawing audiences to these Italian language performances was that much of the repertory was already known through the English companies that had gone before. This style of Italian grand opera traveling with a European star emulated earlier English companies and remained characteristic of opera in America into the twentieth century.

THE SOUTH

During the two decades before the Civil War in the South, the variety and quality of opera companies created an active, brilliant period. The New Orleans of the 1850s saw an emerging kaleidoscope of English, French and Italian operas given by travelling troupes as a highly visible foreground to the consistent backdrop of the resident French company. Italian opera staged by the Havana Company in 1847 was declared the best to date, and high musical standards continued in the Arditi-Devries performances a few years later. Throughout the decade of the 1840s the Seguins had dominated the English opera scene in several extensive Southern tours (New Orleans was their farthest point), with works that had proven successful over time. They gave their great success, Balfe's The Bohemian Girl, an expensive staging in New York at the Park Theater in 1844, one year after its London premiere. This opera was probably performed more than any other in America in the next ten years and continued to thrive with extraordinary success to the end of the century.

Michael Balfe (1808-1870), its composer, was born in Dublin in 1808 and initially earned his living as a violinist, but won much greater recognition when he turned to singing. He studied with Charles Edward Horn in London and then composer Luigi Cherubini in Paris, where he debuted at the Théâtre des Italiens as Figaro in Barber of Seville. Later he sang there in Rossini's Cenerentola with Malibran, whom he later rejoined at Milan's La Scala. On his return to London in 1833 he started composing and produced nearly thirty operas and over 500 other works, many of which are vocal. A strong advocate for establishing an English national opera, Balfe achieved considerable fame in Europe as a singer and was subsequently recognized by his contemporaries as a talented, versatile and productive composer.

The Bohemian Girl, libretto by Alfred Bunn, takes place in Hungary in the early nineteenth century and concerns a noble Polish exile, Thaddeus, who has joined a band of gypsies led by one Devilshoof. Thaddeus falls in love with the youthful Arline, who has been raised by the gypsies, but who is really the daughter of the Governor of Presburg, Count Arnheim. To complete the picture, we soon discover that the Queen of the gypsies also loves Thaddeus. During the Carnival at Presburg Arline is falsely accused of stealing a medallion and brought before Count Arnheim for judgement, at which point he recognizes her as his daughter. Thaddeus and Arline overcome the count's opposition to their marriage, Devilshoof circumvents the evil machinations of the gypsy Queen, and the couple is finally joined in matrimony.

Musically, Balfe's operas rely heavily on the consistent flow of appealing melodic ideas, often easily remembered if not always profound. *The Bohemian Girl* speaks in a relatively conventional harmonic language compared to other works of the time, and its musical structures, interspersed with dialogue, present no surprises. Balfe, however, clearly touched a resounding chord in his audiences, for *The Bohemian Girl* was a huge success in Europe as well as America. One of the immediate measures of this success (aside from the box office receipts) was the number of travesties that appeared in this country such as the blackface version, *The Virginian Girl*, at Nelson Kneass's Ethiopian Burlesque Opera Company and *The Bohea-Man's Girl* at the Olympic Theater. Elsewhere the hit tune "I Dreamt I Dwelt in Marble Halls" was transformed into the wickedly funny "I Dreamt I Had Money to Buy a Shawl."[40]

By the 1850s a variety of troupes had joined the Seguins to spread opera further away from the East Coast. Anne Thillon and James Hudson traveled to Cincinnati, St. Louis, Memphis, Mobile, and New Orleans with Balfe's *The Enchantress* and *The Bohemian Girl*, Rooke's *Amilie, or The Love Test*, plus other works in English translations.[41]

Of more lasting fame was the Richings Opera Company. Organized by English actor-singer Peter Richings and starring his adopted daughter Caroline, the company was touring by 1854. Richings, who had come here from England in 1821, had sung in the premiere of Fry's *Leonora* with the Seguins and managed its much admired staging. Caroline had started out as a pianist, but soon turned to singing, making her debut at Philadelphia's Walnut Street Theater in Donizetti's *The Daughter of the Regiment* in 1852. She would become a well regarded singer in larger cities as well as on the circuits and had attained enough artistic stature for the discriminating Maretzek to choose her to sing Adalgisa in his 1856 production of Norma. A fine actress, Caroline appeared with her father in plays as well as English operas. In 1862 she sang the leading role of Stella in Balfe's opera The Enchantress in New York. The opera ran for eight weeks at Niblo's, firmly established her reputation and was long associated with her. She followed this up with a less successful, if similarly titled work, The Syren. In February 1863, at the New York premiere of Balfe's Satanella, or The Power of Love she accomplished the impressive feat of singing all three major roles: Satanella, the Spirit of Beauty; Julian, a demon page; and Arimane, the master fiend. By the 1870s she was acting as impresario for the touring companies she managed with her husband, tenor Peter Bernard. In addition, she sang in the performances and translated works into English.

Equally well known was the Pyne and Harrison English Opera Company that had premiered George Bristow's opera Rip Van Winkle at Niblo's. Pyne and Harrison's Southern tours swung through Louisville, Mobile, St. Louis, Washington and Richmond as far as New Orleans, while Boston, Baltimore, Pittsburgh and Cincinnati circumscribed their northern circuit.[42] Their repertory in English comprised Auber's Fra Diavolo and The Crown Diamonds, Barber of Seville, Cinderella, La sonnambula, Daughter of the Regiment, The Bohemian Girl and English composer William Wallace's Maritana. Soprano Louisa Pyne and tenor William Harrison had sung leading roles in English operas of Balfe and Wallace at Drury Lane in London before coming to this country and would shortly return to London to take the lead in producing operas by English composers in a city still dominated by Italian works. Critic White found Louisa Pyne's voice "a light soprano of delicious quality . . . and very flexible . . . her execution delicate and finished."[43]

An examination of Charleston, a strong cultural center for some time and favorite theatrical stop for opera companies between the Northeast and New Orleans, illustrates what a variety of opera companies were touring the East Coast and the contemporary if repetitive nature of their repertories. By the 1850s the city was a major shipping and manufacturing center, was developing new banks, had three colleges, a Museum of Natural History, a Library and an Historical Society. For the sake of simplicity we will look at only the beginning and end of the decade.

In the spring of 1850 the increasingly famous Havana Company, with more than ninety artists, including sopranos Fortunata Tedesco, Balbina Steffanone, and tenor Lorenzo Salvi, under conductor Arditi had presented Norma, Lucrezia Borgia and Ernani. Those three works were repeated by an "Italian Opera Company" the next spring, in addition to Donizetti's La Favorita, and Lucia and Mercadante's Il giuramento (The Oath). Some members of that company, now under the name of "Mozart's Don Giovanni Opera Company," returned in December of 1851 with a refurbished repertory that included, appropriately, Don Giovanni and Donizetti's Roberto Devereux. Max Maretzek's Opera Company, in which Rosa Devries was then singing, preceded them in November with offerings of Norma, I puritani, Lucia, Don Pasquale, La sonnambula, Ernani and La Favorita. Two years later, in 1853, Niblo's English Opera Troupe staged The Bohemian Girl, Lucia and La sonnambula, followed in succession by Maretzek for two performances and one night of the Madame D'Angri Opera Company. Italian opera returned to Charleston in 1858 with the Havana Italian Opera Company, which added La traviata (The Strayed One) and L'elisir d'amore to the better known works. That same year the Italian Opera Company with Teresa Parodi and Barili staged the well-known Italian repertory.[44] Also in 1858 the New Orleans English Opera Troupe performed three weeks of La sonnambula, Barber of Seville, Daughter of the Regiment, Bohemian Girl, Il trovatore, Cinderella, and The Beggar's Opera. A year later they returned to be followed by the Sanford Opera Company, which staged a small but familiar English repertory, as did the Cooper English Opera Troupe in 1860.

After Charleston a company might head toward Columbus Georgia's fine theater, Temperance Hall, or Savannah, and include St. Louis and Mobile in their circuit before or after New Orleans. Famous theatrical managers Ludlow and Smith had started the circuit of New Orleans, Mobile and St. Louis in 1837 originally in competition with James Caldwell.

THE WEST COAST

Less populated, less accessible and, until the Gold Rush of 1849, less explored was the West. Boom towns then mushroomed but remained in relative isolation from the East, being accessible only by lengthy sea routes or even lengthier and more dangerous overland trails. San Francisco, however, was introduced to Norma in April 1854 by the indefatigable Anna Bishop, who followed it up with La sonnambula, Don Pasquale and others, but remembering this singer's penchant for giving "selected scenes," it is possible some performances had that format. The same year Anne Thillon sang Cinderella there, recruiting local talent for her supporting cast and probably for an orchestra. More consistent operatic performances began when tenor Eugenio Bianchi and his wife, soprano Giovanna, arrived by way of Mexico in 1857 to become fixtures in San Francisco's musical life. The city's most popular operas during the 1850s were The Daughter of the Regiment (with twenty-three recorded performances), Norma, The Crown Diamonds, and La sonnambula. Performance standards developed slowly, however, as we learn from a complaint by the Daily Bulletin (May 6, 1859) that not only were women's voices lacking in the chorus of Il trovatore but also that the orchestra needed more rehearsals and that the singers used several languages. Finally the Bulletin admonishes that "an improvement would be effected by dispensing with the cow-bell used to signal the orchestra into their places, preparatory to calling up the curtain."[45]

DRAMA AND MUSIC

The decline of comic operas in favor of those on tragic themes is by now striking. Even in those with happy endings such as La sonnambula and The Bohemian Girl in which both heroines manage to marry "up," (the hope of many American girls), the lighter comic touches are few. The focus on hopeless love accompanied by violent death, all enacted in a tumultuous setting, was exemplified in works such as Norma or Lucia. The betrayed Norma ends up on a funeral pyre with her faithless lover. Lucia goes mad, murders her unwanted spouse, and dies before her beloved stabs himself. Although women increasingly occupy a central place around which all else revolves, they are usually in a dependent position with little control over their fate, even in the case of the strong Druid Priestess, Norma. One has only to compare them to some of the Mozart heroines to be struck by the profound difference. By mid-century passion had to be paid for by disaster to the woman. Periods and places chosen as settings are generally post-classical, except Norma, but distant, stretching from early nineteenth-century Hungary back to fifteenth-century Spain. As exceptions, Rip Van Winkle and La sonnambula look back to the pastoral village of eighteenth-century opera. A distant past and place, however, became more attractive and prevalent as current mores were played out, supported, and justified.

The change in Rossini's melodic style has already been noted, a change influenced by the different type of singers for whom he wrote. Although Rossini's enormous prestige had a stultifying effect on many composers, musical individuality did evolve and become evident in works of Donizetti and Bellini. The latter developed a fluid, ornamented vocal line of a distinctive character, of which the most famous example may be "Casta Diva" from Norma, while the former tended toward rousing tunes with strong repetitive rhythms and rather basic harmonies. We find that the older "dry" recitative of Rossini has been replaced by arioso style, that is, it is more lyrical, and ensembles have been placed at crucial dramatic points. Thus the intensely conflicted feelings that arise during the confrontation about Lucia's marriage are expressed in the famous Sextet in Lucia, rather than in an aria by the prima donna. The chorus has become an indispensable element for both composers as well as for Verdi. Orchestration in Bellini and Donizetti maintains its emphasis on the strings, but with Verdi we find heavier orchestration, with much more use of brass and much greater striving for atmospheric colors. We hear this in the Anvil Chorus of Il trovatore, or, in a more subtle fashion, in the storm music in the last act of Rigoletto with its wordless chorus.

These stylistic changes clearly affected singers who had to adapt to the new requirements. They had to sing louder to be heard over heavier orchestration, they had to bring greater intensity to sustain broader vocal lines and they were no longer consistently called on to ornament melodies creatively as had been customary earlier. Besides all of that, the new type of recitative required a different approach to the projection of the character, which formerly had been developed largely through the arias, with recitative often viewed simply as "filler." Virtuosity was certainly still essential, as witness the numerous "mad scenes" in Bellini and Donizetti that exploited it, but individual improvisation was less important and vocal technique had to be rethought.

CONCLUSIONS

Structurally, two closely connected events had had a telling effect on opera: the emergence of a new style of manager with new business methods and the foreign language repertory that accompanied him. A Maretzek or Ullmann could not depend on the local stock company to fill in roles in the more complex Italian repertory they promoted, although traveling English troupes still could and did. As companies became larger and more costly and their travel routes expanded, the orchestra or chorus might still be amplified by local talent, but probably less so than in the past. So more people had to be transported at greater expense. Famous foreign stars who saw America as a new arena for their artistic triumphs and fresh financial gain were necessary for the major parts and even some minor ones. The new style of managers recognized early on the not-so-subtle interaction of wealth, social hierarchy, exclusivity, and imported foreign language opera and singers. This precluded any possibility, if it existed, of an acceptance of works by Americans in English. Meantime the publicity techniques of Barnum and Ullmann became standard.

Musically, a sea change had taken place during the 1840s and '50s in which the Italian vocal style of Bellini and Donizetti had risen to the top of the musical heap. Rossini's <u>Cinderella</u> and <u>Barber</u>, with their cadenzas and roulades, may have raised the curtain, but it was the longer lines of <u>Norma</u> and <u>Il trovatore</u> that brought it down. Translated arias, even when changed or shortened, maintained their lyrical melodic lines with their elaborate ornamentation supported by relatively simple accompaniments designed to underline rather than compete with the voice. This same style, with individual adaptions to be sure, appears in Balfe's works as well as Fry's. In Balfe's case this was to be expected, given his Italian training and his rather extensive experience with Italian opera as a singer. Likewise, the influence of bel canto on Fry seems almost inevitable, given his admiration for and extensive performance experience with Norma.

By the early 1860s the imminence of the Civil War cast a pall over most theatrical and musical life. In Charleston all interest was focused on the political situation, as South Carolina seceded, and the theater was forgotten. Adelina Patti chose the moment to head for Europe while Clara Louise Kellogg, also at the beginning of her career, chose to stay here, but noted that the times were hard for opera and remained so throughout the war.

NOTES

1. George Clinton Densmore Odell, Annals of the New York Stage (New York: Columbia University Press, 1927-1937), vol. 6, p. 478. H. Earle Johnson, Operas on American Subjects (New York: Coleman-Ross Co., 1964), p. 30.

2. William W. Clapp, A Record of the Boston Stage (New York: Greenwood Press, 1969), p. 42.

3. Alexis de Tocqueville, Democracy in America, ed. J. P. Mayer (New York: Doubleday & Company, Inc., 1969), p. 432.

4. The New Harvard Dictionary of Music, ed. Don Michael Randel (Cambridge, MA: The Belknap Press of Harvard University Press, 1986), p. 192.

5. Christopher Hatch, "Music for America: A Critical Controversy of the 1850s," American Quarterly XIV/4 (1962), pp.578-586, sets forth the facets and complexity of these attitudes.

6. John Smith Kendall, The Golden Age of the New Orleans Theater (Baton Rouge: Louisiana State University Press, 1952), pp. 184-185 notes an earlier Havana Opera Company that sang in New Orleans in 1842; Katherine Keenan Preston, "Travelling Opera Troupes in the United States, 1825-1860" (Ph.D. dissertation, City University of New York,

1989), pp. 234-236 cites a different Havana Opera Company on a tour that ends in New York in 1843; W. G. Armstrong, Record of the Opera in Philadelphia (New York: AMS, 1976), p. 47 notes performances of this company in Philadelphia in the same year.

7. Max Maretzek, Revelation of an Opera Manager in Nineteenth-Century America. Crotchets & Quavers, Sharps & Flats. (New York: Dover, 1968), p. 151.

8. William W. Clapp, A Record of the Boston Stage (New York: Greenwood Press, 1969), p. 445.

9. David Kimbell, Italian Opera (Cambridge: Cambridge University Press, 1991), p. 496.

10. Armstrong, Record of the Opera in Philadelphia, p. 56.

11. Vera Brodsky Lawrence, Strong on Music: The New York Music Scene in the Days of George Templeton Strong, 1836-1875, Vol. I, Resonances 1836-1850 (New York: Oxford University Press, 1988), p. 482.

12. Ibid., pp. 470-471.

13. Peter George Buckley, "To the Opera House: Culture and Society in New York City, 1820-1860." (Ph.D. dissertation, State University of New York at Stony Brook, 1984), p. 299.

14. Maretzek, Revelations of an Opera Manager, p. 59.

15. Henry C. Lahee, Grand Opera in America (Boston: L. C. Page & Co., 1902), p. 97.

16. Clara Louise Kellogg, Memoirs of an American Prima Donna (New York: G. P. Purnam's Sons, The Knickerbocker Press, 1913), p. 41.

17. Maretzek, Revelations of an Opera Manager, p. 33.

18. Armstrong, Record of the Opera in Philadelphia, p. 59.

19. Dwight's Journal of Music, October 2, 1858.

20. Meyerbeer later incorporated four numbers from Feldlager into his opera L'Étoile du Nord, (The Star of the North).

21. Odell, Annals, Vol. 6, pp. 87-88.

22. Richard Jackson, Democratic Souvenirs: An Historical Anthology of Nineteenth-Century American Music (New York: C. F. Peters Corp., 1988), p. 294.

23. Vera Brodsky Lawrence, "William Henry Fry's Messianic Yearnings: Eleven Lectures 1852-53," American Music VII/4 (1989), pp. 382-411.

24. George F. Bristow, Rip Van Winkle, ed. Steven Ledbetter (New York: Da Capo Press, 1991), p. ix.

25. Delmer Dalzell Rogers, "Nineteenth Century Music in New York as Reflected in the Career of George Frederick Bristow (Ph. D. dissertation, University of Michigan, 1967), p. 164.

26. An Italian version was planned by Maretzek as a revival in 1865.

27. Charles Hamm, Yesterdays: Popular Song in America (New York: W. W. Norton & Company, 1979), pp. 78-82.

28. David Grimsted, Melodrama Unveiled: American Theater and Culture, 1800-1850 (Chicago: University of Chicago Press, 1968), p. 238.

29. Lawrence, Strong on Music, p. 133.

30. Henry C. Lahee, Annals of Music in America (New York: AMS Press reprint, 1969), p. 66.

31. L. M. Lerner, "The Rise of the Impresario: Bernard Ullmann and the Transformation of Musical Culture in Nineteenth Century America," (Ph.D. dissertation University of Wisconsin, 1970). This source provided most of the information on Ullmann.

32. New York Times, January 7, 1853.

33. The Century, XXIII (May 1882), p. 37.

34. Maretzek, Revelations of an Opera Manager, p. 37.

35. Luigi Arditi, My Reminiscences (New York: Dodd Mead, 1896), p. 73.

36. John C. Swan, ed., Music in Boston (Boston: Trustees of the Public Library of the City of Boston, 1977), p. 75.

37. Odell, Annals, vol.5, pp. 51-52.

38. Arditi, My Reminiscences, p. 17.

39. Thomas G. Kaufman, "The Arditi Tour: The Midwest Gets Its First Real Taste of Italian Opera," Opera Quarterly, III/3 (1986/87), pp. 39-52. This article provided much of the information on the tour.

40. Lawrence, Strong on Music, p. 328.

41. Preston, "Travelling Opera Troupes," pp. 506-507.

42. Ibid., chapter 6.

43. The Century, vol. XXIV, p. 198.

44. W. Stanley Hoole, The Ante-Bellum Charleston Theatre (Tuscaloosa: University of Alabama Press, 1946), chapter 6.

45. Cornel Lengyel, ed., Music of the Gold Rush Era: History of Music in San Francisco Series (New York: AMS Press Reprint, 1972), vol. 1, p. 136.

5

Contemporary European Opera: 1865–1883

Do you know the country where the lemon trees blossom?
Among dark leaves the golden oranges glow.
A gentle breeze from blue skies drifts.
The myrtle is still, and the laurel stands high.
Do you know it well?
There, there would I go with you, my beloved.

Goethe
Mignon's song from Whilhelm Meister

Jacques Offenbach, a prolific composer of light operas, arrived in America in 1876 to conduct concerts in celebrations of our centennial in New York and Philadelphia and then to tour. By this time in his career, Offenbach keenly grasped what was essential for opera's success through his extensive experience in opera production and direction in Paris. As he aptly put it,

In New York there is no permanent opera, no permanent opéra-comique, nor even any operetta theatre which is sure of two years of life . . . . The directors and their companies are all nomads. Most of the artists are just visitors borrowed from the Old World, coming for one season only and then leaving."[1]

This observation clearly described the activity and style of traveling companies during the eighteen-year period from the end of the Civil War to the building of the Metropolitan Opera House in 1883. That event focused opera more intensely on one place, New

York, and garnered the financial support required to develop a more stable economic base.

THE MUSICAL VISTA

Language continued to be a distinctive factor among companies, for while some of these "nomads" espoused an English repertory, others sang only in Italian and a few in German. The idea that opera should be performed in the language originally set by the composer would not become common until seven consecutive seasons of Wagner had been performed at the Metropolitan. As operatic tensions focused more directly on the English, Italian-French and newly arrived German repertories, none of which, as Offenbach observed, had a stable home, a deadly competition prevailed, allowing few to survive for long. A cluster of troupes that translated European operas into English continued during the 1870s. They made newer works available to a large audience, often including light operas as part of their attraction. Companies with Italian trained singers promoted the older Italian repertory or works translated into Italian such as Faust (French), Lohengrin (German), or The Talisman (English). This made everything easier for Italian casts and helped sustain the myth that this was the only language appropriate and possible for opera. Concurrently a repertory of Gilbert and Sullivan operettas, Viennese operettas, and sophisticated French opéra-bouffe appeared. As a slowly developing background to this fragmented vista, interest grew in an emerging group of German operas. That interest would flower into enthusiasm by the mid-1880s.

This colorful kaleidoscope kept shifting in the postwar decades as new companies, or reconstituted companies with new names, arose often to flourish briefly and disappear as managers continued to vie for stars and audiences. Whoever the star or manager and whatever the name, all companies traveled.

AFTERMATH OF THE CIVIL WAR

In general, managers, stars, and troupes had retreated to Europe for the duration of the Civil War, realizing that the country's entire attention was riveted on this painful internal battle with little time for musical diversions. The war's physical damage was of course greatest in the South, where operatic centers such as Richmond, Charleston, and New Orleans suffered heavily under fire, bombardment, or blockade. Near chaos reigned by the end of the war, for the whole fabric of Southern society had been torn apart. A generation of young men had been lost and the emotional damage was devastating. It was a changed world in which the ensuing Reconstruction, although well intentioned, only created new problems and perpetuated the pain of defeat. Despite New Orleans' political unrest and tumult in the five years after the Civil War, by the decade of the 1870s, a smattering of Italian, English and French comic opera was being given sporadically by traveling companies. While the North was equally devastated by the loss of life and the bitterness war engenders, victory somewhat tempered such feelings. In addition, the commercial sectors of society such as transportation, manufacturing, and agriculture remained relatively intact with the economic and political life of the cities themselves much less disrupted.

Transportation, particularly railroads and steamships, became an important element in operatic expansion. Railroads covered 35,000 miles at the end of the War and would increase to five times that by the turn of the century, weaving a vast network that interlocked cities and towns. By the late 1860s steamships were crossing the ocean faster and more safely with greater comfort and better accommodations than previously, although the trip still could take up to several weeks.

As attractive advantages of immigration were advertised abroad, the influx of new citizens continued to grow in reaction to an increased European population, political unrest and the upheavals caused by the industrial revolution. Castle Garden, where Jenny Lind had first performed, had been revamped in 1855 as a reception center to serve the ever growing numbers of new immigrants. A predominant number were Catholic, and many came under a system of "contract" labor that was similar to the "indentured" servitude of the eighteenth century. Those who came in the twenty-five years following the Civil War were primarily from northern Europe and the British Isles. A large number of these were Germans, a factor that would color our musical life for the next sixty years, as names such as Steinway and Damrosch became as well known in the musical world as Rockefeller and Astor, both likewise of German descent, became in the business world.

The enthusiasm of the German immigrants for concerts, singing societies, and music in general was a distinguishing group characteristic. Singer David Bispham reported that as a youth growing up in Philadelphia, most of the open-air concerts were in the German parts of the city, where he first heard the great Hungarian violinist Eduard Remenyi. Most cities with much of a German population had one or more amateur choruses, such as the Philadelphia Maennerchor (founded in 1835), or New York's Arion Society, or the Liederkranz Society in which William Steinway was an active member. Choral competitions, called Saengerfests, gathered a number of the groups together from surrounding cities to sing mainly German works in festivals that might last a week. Participants could thus preserve their German language and culture as well as enjoy the social activity of the accompanying dinners and dances.

The British heritage, although less dominant than earlier, was still clearly in evidence and manifested itself in various ways. Pastor Dr. Josiah Strong of Cincinnati would reach a broad audience in his best seller, Our Country (first published in 1885), which directly proclaimed: "The Anglo-Saxon . . . is divinely commissioned to be . . . his brother's keeper, . . . God . . . is . . . preparing in our civilization the die with which to stamp the nations."[2] Individuals began to cast longing backward glances at their British heritage, and author Henry James and painter James Whistler actually took up residence in England in the second half of the century. Groups such as the Colonial Dames of America, the Mayflower Society, and others sprang up and were cultivated as a means of identifying one's "own sort" and as badges of social distinction. An extreme example of a turn to British aristocracy occurred in the 1880s when William Astor became the first American "peer" in England.

OPERA IN ENGLISH

In the decade after the Civil War opera companies sprang up, flowered and faded as they traversed the railroad networks of the Northeast and Midwest. Of the many that sang opera in English, three are particularly noteworthy because of their quality, ubiquity, and longevity: Richings, Parepa-Rosa, and Kellogg. These troupes were all managed by women who had considerable administrative as well as musical talents. They did a large part of the direction and planning of productions, most arranging of musical scores and translating of librettos, and performed the major roles. The Chicago Tribune noted:

> These three troupes [referring to Richings, Parepa-Rosa and Kellogg] demonstrated that English opera could be given in a manner worthy of comparison with the Italian and German traditions. . . . Their repertoires . . . of German, French and Italian . . . were put on the stage with careful attention to details. The performances were in every way as interesting as those under the management of Grau, Maretzek and Mapleson. In short, they were meritorious, popular, and successful.[3]

The Richings company has already been discussed, but not the Parepa-Rosa or the Kellogg. Scottish born Euphrosyne Parepa was the niece of Edward Seguin, star of the 1840s. Her mother, Elizabeth Seguin, was also a singer and became her daughter's vocal teacher. After singing opera and concerts in Europe from 1855-1865, Euphrosyne came to the United States to tour with Theodore Thomas's orchestra and married one of its violinists, Carl Rosa. Over the next few years she sang in the standard Italian fare of Lucia, Trovatore, Norma, and the like. She and her husband then formed the Parepa-Rosa English Opera Company in 1869 to continue the Seguin family tradition of opera in English and toured for several years with a company of as many as one hundred. After it was disbanded the couple returned to England, where Rosa would continue some sort of involvement with opera for many years. During their American tours the company included her cousin Edward Seguin, his wife Zelda (both later in Emma Abbott's company), Rose Hersée, William Castle, and others, as well as a strong orchestra and chorus with Rosa conducting. The discriminating Arditi praised Rosa in his Reminiscences as a fine conductor, a good organizer and shrewd businessman. The Parepa-Rosa company used better translations and musical arrangements of the popular Italian works than those used by earlier English troupes. In 1871, the last year they played in Cincinnati, their varied repertory leaned much more toward non-serious works than tragedy. It consisted of: W. V. Wallace's Maritana; Balfe's Satanella and The Bohemian Girl; Auber's Fra Diavolo; Donizetti's Daughter of the Regiment and Lucrezia Borgia; Rossini's La gazza ladra (The Thieving Magpie); Verdi's Un ballo in maschera (A Masked Ball); and Mozart's Don Giovanni and The Marriage of Figaro.[4] Dwight had earlier praised this last as a highlight and two years before had remarked on the performance of Martha in Chicago as especially pleasing.

The consistent place in company repertories of Friedrich von Flotow's Martha is noteworthy because it illustrates both the ability of the prima donna to sustain a work over time and a type of opera that would only flourish in the particular climate of its period. From its first performance at Niblo's Garden in 1852 in English rather than the original German, it was repeatedly staged by many troupes. The leading soprano role was cultivated by famous prima donnas Anna de La Grange and Pauline Colson in the 1850s and later by Adelina Patti, Clara Louise Kellogg, Christine Nilsson, and Marcella Sembrich. The score includes "The Last Rose of Summer," an old street ballad that was borrowed and interpolated, a tenor aria "Oh, How Fair" that became popular, and some tuneful ensembles that give life to the rather slim story and doubtless charmed audiences.[5] The libretto presents the tale of an aristocratic lady and a friend who pose as servants to two farmers. The commoner falls in love with the aristocrat, and the rest of the opera winds its way to the revelation of the commoner's aristocratic parentage, his title and estate. Once more, a concealed aristocratic origin (or mistaken identity) formed the linchpin of the libretto, as it had in masterpieces or lesser works from The Marriage of Figaro to The Devil's Bridge and The Bohemian Girl. In the end love triumphs, a favorite fantasy fulfilled, and prima donnas and audiences loved it.

Clara Louise Kellogg's Company introduced operas in English, such as Martha, Mignon, and Faust, to many audiences. Singer David Bispham recalled those performances with pleasure and also remembered Zelda Seguin, when she sang with the Richings-Bernard Company, as one of the best Carmens he ever heard--a high compliment from one singer to another and testimony to the high quality of singers in these troupes. Kellogg, who later married Carl Strakosch, the nephew of manager Maurice, had a very substantial European and American reputation when she embarked on her English Opera Company venture with C. D. Hess in 1873. She believed, she later wrote, that her enterprise was successful in two ways: in introducing fine music to large groups unacquainted with it before and in giving a number of young American singers their start in successful careers.[6] Her memoirs reveal practices at the time of the Civil War that give the special flavor of that time:

> we were also genuinely moved by the contagious glow that pervaded the country and the times, . . . For example, we were barbarous enough to put in sundry American national airs . . . and this reminds me that about the same period Isabella Hinckley even sang "The Star Spangled Banner" in the middle of a performance of Il Barbiere.[7]

Kellogg herself made new translations of the Italian, French or German texts, and oversaw the productions as to directing, scenery, costuming and rehearsals. This energetic and determined woman gave careful attention to all details. Her solid training, intelligence, and European experience enabled her to create convincing performances that drew in enthusiastic audiences despite some initial, and inevitable, criticism concerning the suitability of the English language for opera. The repertory included Thomas' Mignon, Meyerbeer's The Star of the North, The Flying Dutchman, Faust, The Marriage of Figaro, Lily o' Killarney (written for Kellogg by Julius Benedict), as well as Balfe's The Rose of

Castille, The Bohemian Girl (which she considered poor, but says always filled the house), and The Talisman, based on a Scott novel. Kellogg called this opera, somewhat reminiscent of Meyerbeer, Balfe's only real grand opera. And indeed it was first put on in truly grand style at London's Drury Lane with a stellar cast of Christine Nilsson, Italo Campanini and Marie Roze. Marguerite in Faust, which Kellogg created under Maretzek in this country in Italian, was probably her most famous role. She was twenty at the time and describes how strange the music seemed at first, since it was not in the older Italian style of a Bellini or Donizetti in which she had been trained. Also she had no models to follow in developing the visual aspects of the role, but she managed through her diligent efforts to present a convincing, well-rounded portrayal and her success was considerable. Faust would become one of the most often performed pieces of the century.

A special facet to this "Opera in English" movement that illustrates an aspect of the tenor of the times was added by singer Emma Abbott, a young woman from modest circumstances, who was encouraged by Kellogg to pursue a serious singing career and headed a touring company for thirteen years. She made her operatic debut at Covent Garden in London, but her contract was cancelled when she refused to appear in Verdi's La traviata because she found it immoral. Abbott never completely rejected, or outgrew, her rather restrictive sense of morality to move into the larger cultural world that opera could have offered. Eventually in 1878, when she too produced opera in English here, she staged abridged versions of standard works and would interject "Nearer My God to Thee" (and probably other hymns) in Faust and La sonnambula and "Home, Sweet Home" almost anywhere. If one considers this in the context of the continuing habit, at least outside major cities, of a general use of interpolations and some obvious examples of borrowings, one can see that Abbott's interjections, although inappropriate by our standards, were less so in her time. To her credit she, like Kellogg and other women managers mentioned, oversaw or handled all aspects of production as well as being the star performer in attractive stagings that were comprehensible and solid musically for what they were. The famous and frequently advertised "Abbott's Kiss", which attracted considerable attention, also indicates her sense of public relations, but what exactly distinguished the kiss remains a mystery. In 1872 she opened the newly remodeled Staub's Opera House in Knoxville, Tennessee, with Martha and received many curtain calls. Between 1878 and 1890 her company opened thirty-five new opera houses, mainly in the West and Midwest--an impressive number. One of the most lavish must have been the Tabor Opera House in Denver with its brocaded seats and walls of panelled mahogany, which Abbott christened with Wallace's Maritana in 1881. Tabor, his fortunes and his love affair with Baby Doe, became the subject of the Douglas Moore opera The Ballad of Baby Doe, more than a half a century later.

OPERETTAS

Another aspect of opera in English so striking that it calls for comment were the operettas of Gilbert and Sullivan. These scintillating satires gained a following in England and in America comparable to that which The Beggar's Opera and the Italian intermezzi, such as La serva padrona, had received in their respective countries during the eighteenth century. The first American performance of H.M.S. Pinafore took place in Boston in 1878 and thus began a phenomenal musical success story. W. S. Gilbert, a lawyer, and Arthur Sullivan, a recognized composer and close friend of the Prince of Wales, had collaborated earlier to produce Trial by Jury. That success was not immediately repeated with Pinafore, partly because the latter vigorously poked fun at British traits and customs. If, however, the British found this farce objectionable, the Americans delighted in it. Former prime minister Disraeli stated that he had "never seen anything so bad as Pinafore," and Londoners generally reacted adversely to the mockery of class distinctions and lampooning of social hypocrisy.[8] These were the very elements that Americans enjoyed and made Pinafore such a hit from the beginning. The wonderfully zany humor of the libretto that turned the world inside out, the clever cohesion of text to music, and the easily remembered songs had immediate appeal. Amateur as well as professional groups picked it up so that simultaneous performances flooded the country, and Americans fell into the grip of the so-called "Pinafore mania." No international copyright law existed, and pirated versions flourished.[9]

Another type of operetta was the French opéra-bouffe, which became popular in the decade of the 1870s. Jacob Grau, uncle of Maurice Grau, later manager at the Metropolitan Opera, introduced many of these French works with their limited dialogue, topical satire, humor, stereotypic characters and engaging music. Their structure of arias, recitatives and ensembles, resembles in its outward trappings that of Italian opera, but the music was generally less substantial. Jacques Offenbach's La Grande Duchesse de Gérolstein, first done in New York in 1867, was one of the most popular. We find it in Philadelphia in February 1868 for ten nights,[10] in spring and fall stagings in Cincinnati in 1868[11] and for the ensuing ten or twelve years a fairly consistent work for various "French" opera companies. It managed to enter the repertory of some companies that performed opera in English, notably that of Mrs. Alice Oates. Offenbach's Orphée aux Enfers (Orpheus in the Underworld) and La Belle Hélène (The Beautiful Helen) achieved a more limited popularity. Important facets of the success of these French opéras-bouffes were the excellence of the performers and the well designed and rehearsed presentations. Offenbach was a thoroughly experienced theater composer whose works came here usually with the original music unchanged and often with musicians who had performed the works in Paris.[12] Thus the piece could be seen to best advantage. One of the most popular singers was Marie Aimée, who made her New York debut in 1870 in Offenbach's Barbe-Bleue, usually was managed by Grau and in a few years had her own touring company. Translations of Offenbach's works became popular with amateur groups, as would works by Gilbert and Sullivan by the end of the 1870s.

One operetta by an American that achieved noticeable dissemination was The Doctor of Alcantara by European-trained Julius Eichberg. A violinist who studied at the Brussels Conservatory, Eichberg settled in Boston in 1859 and founded the Boston Conservatory in 1867. First given in Boston in 1862, the operetta was taken up by the Richings Company and appears in

Cincinnati in 1873 in the repertory of the Seguin Grand English Opera Company. The Seguins had doubtless learned the piece when they sang with Richings in earlier seasons.

Opera in English became a positive musical experience and the introduction for many to standard European works in their own language. Doubtless, for some it also served as preparation for foreign language performances by the many other traveling troupes. More important, opera and operetta added a dimension to the musical lives of many people.

ITALIAN AND OTHER EUROPEAN OPERA

Another part of the moving operatic caravan was occupied by the companies under older, better known managers promoting opera in Italian, French or German. We find the Strakosch brothers, Jacob Grau, and Max Maretzek heading troupes that often competed and occasionally combined in their efforts to win audiences. Max Strakosch's perambulations of several seasons serve as an example. His staging of Il trovatore, Don Pasquale and Il barbiere di Siviglia in Philadelphia in March 1870 was undoubtedly a part of a New York run that preceded or followed a route including Baltimore and Washington. The following year found him in the Boston segment of a tour in October with more of the "old favorites," a euphemism for oft-repeated Italian works. Strakosch and his brother Maurice joined with their rival Maretzek the next year in Cincinnati to form the Grand Italian Opera Company with such staples as Lucia, La sonnambula, Faust, and one novelty (meaning a newer work): Thomas's Mignon. Maretzek would again join Strakosch and hire most of the singers in London when they managed the Lucca-Kellogg company in 1872. By 1875 famous stars such as Mmes. Albani, Tietjens and Carreño (and her husband Tagliapetra), all worked under Strakosch's operatic management, offering mainly Italian works with occasional shifts to the French repertory such as Faust, Les Huguenots (The Huguenots), and the new Mignon.

Mignon (premiered in Paris in 1866) is interesting not only for facets of its origin and performance, but also for the familiar elements of its plot. Based on a German work, Goethe's novel Wilhelm Meister, but set by the French composer Ambroise Thomas and often sung in Italian, it shares this type of mixed lineage with several other works. Librettists Barbier and Carré had also written the texts for Gounod's Faust and Roméo et Juliette and for Thomas's Hamlet. While they turned to the monumental Goethe and Shakespeare as sources, they "adapted" the originals to the point of reducing them to mere sketches of the powerful dramas, thus conforming to current French taste and the general model of the earlier style of Meyerbeer-Scribe collaborations. In Mignon the profound aspects of Goethe's work are discarded and a happy ending provided along with Thomas's brilliant, somewhat facile music and several striking arias. The overall result is somewhat bland. Familiar elements of the plot consist of Mignon's ignorance of her noble parentage, her abduction as a child by gypsies (shades of The Bohemian Girl), her befriending of an old minstrel who turns out to be her father, and other such devices. Bland or facile, the opera attained immense popularity in France as well as in this country. Italian was the operative language for these French and German operas unless circumstances dictated otherwise, as when the cast knew only the original language. Meyerbeer's L'Africaine (The African Woman), for instance, was translated from French into Italian and staged at the New York's Academy of Music eight months after its Paris premiere. Six months later Strakosch presented it in Chicago with Amalia Patti (Adelina's talented, but crippled sister) with the "Ghioni and Susini Grand Italian Opera Company" which he managed. Armstrong commented on it at the first performance in Philadelphia as a "fine opera, . . . orchestration beautiful," and it joined the list of Meyerbeer's seemingly ever popular works.

L'Africaine (premiered in Paris in 1865) was Meyerbeer's last opera and perhaps his best.[13] He worked over it for many years, but died before it was performed. Its five long acts, besides a ballet, are set in sixteenth-century Lisbon, on the high seas, and in a strange land beyond Africa. It relates a tale of the explorer Vasco da Gama and two African prisoners he has brought back from a voyage. One of them is a Hindu queen who falls in love with Vasco, who loves a Spanish lady, who in turn is loved by the cruel president of the Royal Council of Portugal. A shipwreck, a massacre, an off-stage execution and the final double suicide offered plenty of opportunity for the dramatic, violent action and contrasting effects used so successfully by the Meyerbeer-Scribe team. The clergy is cast in a poor light in L'Africaine as in some of his other works, for any view of historical events was molded to support the current popular political point of view in Paris.

A major element in Meyerbeer's operas was the stage setting, or the spectacle, which must have been a scene designer's dream. Here, besides the rolling ship in Act III, there is the Prison of the Inquisition of Act II, the Temple of Brahma and Palace of Act IV, and the Queen's Garden of Act V.

Musically L'Africaine is a long, complex score that depends heavily on ensembles rather than arias at its most dramatic moments. Meyerbeer's arias, nonetheless, are as brilliant as his choral pieces are grand in scope. Despite a fundamentally eclectic style he was capable of novel orchestral and spectacular visual effects within his elaborate musical tapestries. The results appealed successfully to audiences of the time and were praised by many contemporaries. Even the hypercritical Berlioz admired Les Huguenots unstintingly.[14] Now, however, these operas seem dated and faded period pieces.

MAPLESON

A new impresario, Colonel J. H. Mapleson (1830-1901), appeared on the scene in 1878 to occupy the center of the stage until a few years after the Metropolitan Opera House opened. For promoters of Italian opera this was a period in which the "star" or the "personality" overshadowed the works staged, a point of view of central importance in Mapleson's thinking. This gentleman had gained his experience in London, where he managed some of the major theaters for a number of years. He was a man who always wore a fresh rose in his buttonhole, knew when and how to kiss his prima donna's hand, often that of Adelina Patti, and could cool, if not control, the continuous simmering jealousies among his singers. His conductor, Arditi, who had worked under many managers, assessed the Colonel as the most astute of impresarios.[15]

Mapleson specialized in all-star casts and ambitious, extensive railroad tours such as the first he undertook in 1878, which included 164 performances staged by a company of 140. He left London at the end of August with a chorus of sixty, a group of dancers, Arditi as conductor, and his soloists. These included Hungarian soprano Etelka Gerster, whose voice was described as "a pure soprano . . . even, penetrating and exceedingly delicate . . . [she] sings with ease and exquisite finish," and soprano Minnie Hauk, the American who became famous for her Carmen.[16] Contraltos were Mme. Trebelli-Bettini and American Alwina Valleria, first tenor Italo Campanini, baritones Antonio Galassi and Giuseppe Del Puente, and Alan J. Foli, an Irishman, the bass. They opened at the Academy in New York with Minnie Hauk in La traviata, and three nights later Mapleson's London theater opened its season. He was now managing concurrent troupes in London and America and as costumes, properties and singers sailed back and forth across the ocean, the nineteenth-century brand of international opera was underway.

Besides New York, their tour included Boston, Chicago, St. Louis, Cincinnati, Philadelphia, Baltimore, and Washington, as they enacted Carmen, Lucia, La sonnambula, Faust, as staples, with less frequent performances of Lohengrin, Il talismano (The Talisman), Il trovatore, Bellini's I puritani and a few others. One of Mapleson's greatest successes on these tours was with the Opera Festival in Cincinnati in which he participated from the beginning. He opened the second Festival with Patti, his great "drawing card" (as he called her), in Les Huguenots. This was followed by Faust, Carmen, Fidelio, and then William Tell, The Magic Flute (in Italian), Lohengrin (in Italian), Il trovatore, and Aida, an acclaimed Patti role. They then went on to Detroit, Buffalo, Cleveland, Syracuse, Albany, and New York, adding Mignon, Rigoletto, Ernani, L'Africaine, and later a revival of Robert le Diable to their performances. In New York, the next year, Mapleson offered one of his famous all-star casts when Patti and Gerster appeared as Valentine and Marguerite de Valois in Les Huguenots with famous tenor Nicolini (Patti's husband) as Raoul and the acclaimed Galassi as St. Bris.

REPERTORY AND SINGERS

The hit of the season had been Carmen with the magnetic Minnie Hauk (1851-1929), who had created the role in both London and New York. This vibrant singer had made her American debut when she was barely sixteen and shortly thereafter sang leading roles under Maretzek in New York and Boston. Subsequently she left for Europe, under the protective wing of her mother (as Kellogg had done), for study and to build a career. By her return ten years later, she had become a major star who had achieved great success in Paris, Berlin, Vienna, Moscow, and London. She said she loved to sing Rosina (Barber of Seville) and Marie (Daughter of the Regiment), a work admired by Mendelssohn, but found Lucia, Amina (La sonnambula) and Linda (Linda di Chamounix) "milk and water" roles.[17] A versatile singing actress, particularly acclaimed for roles as varied as her fiery Carmen and her ethereal Elsa in Lohengrin, Hauk's voice was described as "especially round, full, and resonant, and showing that clear ringing bell-like quality of tone that . . . made her famous the world over."[18]

In the review of a fall performance of Carmen in 1878 in New York, John Dwight reported that the plot was very disturbing to the audience and the music full of strains of Auber, Verdi, Offenbach and Wagner.[19] The original Paris audience had also found the story of this vital villainess, who disregarded accepted morality, upsetting. She was a dramatic change from the usually passive and virtuous heroine, the receptacle of male love. Even Violetta in La traviata evidenced self-doubt and after renouncing her immoral past had died miserable and remorseful. The depiction of gypsies and smugglers as human beings rather than stereotypes was also disconcerting, no less the disintegration without redemption of Don José's character. Bizet, although he had actually softened the Carmen of the original novel by Mérimée, had introduced a new kind of realism into opera that reflected the current literary trend in France toward the "naturalism" of Guy de Maupassant and Emile Zola. Their short stories aimed at capturing a powerful moment of truth, while novels such as Zola's Nana became an almost sociological document of life. In Carmen the characters and final murder onstage were unheard of at the Paris Opéra-Comique, which was viewed as a "family" theater to which one could bring one's wife and daughters.[20] Carmen succeeded largely because of the extraordinary performance and determination of the leading singers, especially the first Carmen, Célestine Galli-Marié. Besides hearing strains of Verdi and Wagner in this colorful and exotic music with its Spanish flavor, Dwight observed "since Aida, I have heard no new opera which has so impressed me with a sense of its composer's originality and with its own freshness." and notes the discriminating use of a recurrent motif. By the time Mapleson arrived at the second Cincinnati Opera Festival in 1882 he claims that Carmen and Fidelio each drew audiences of about 8,000, that the chorus and orchestra were superb, and the audience fashionably dressed, always an important element for Mapleson.[21]

Adelina Patti, famous for her Aida, Gilda and Violetta, usually accompanied Mapleson on his tours, which continued until the spring of 1886. On her appearance in La traviata in 1883 one reviewer had noted that: "One might as well attempt to criticize and analyze the warbling of the nightingale as to discover defects in her voice. Her notes are pure as silver; her vocalization marvelous, and she possesses the rare power of imparting expression to her notes."[22] Her acting was equally acclaimed and with her elaborate costumes and jewels she put on a good show. When she sang in La traviata (one of her most admired roles) under Mapleson in 1883 at the Academy of Music, the major rival to the newly-founded Metropolitan Opera, her costume was thus described: "In the first act she wore a pair of mammoth solitaires, a glittering dog-collar formed of squares of diamonds, a girdle to match, a diamond-studded fan-chain, three sparkling bracelets on each arm, half a dozen ornaments in her hair."[23] She was clearly more interested in her own performance and reception as the star than how well the company or ensemble worked together. Her habit of rarely attending rehearsals had been initiated by her brother-in-law Strakosch when she was still in her 'teens to save her energy for the performance. He would stand in for her at the rehearsal and then explain any changes that had been made. As time went on, and Strakosch was no longer at her side, she continued the practice. This meant that she might only learn of any changes at the last minute, or she might be appearing with new singers for the first time without any rehearsal. Despite Richard Grant White's opinion that she was a fine but not extraordinary singer, many judged her to be in the first rank of international singers of her day. She knew her value to Mapleson and demanded her salary of $5,000 a performance (enormous in its day) up front, before she went on stage: no money, no Patti. Mapleson made sure her arrivals in New York had plenty of publicity, complete with large crowds, boats going out to greet her arrival from Europe, bands and general fanfare, and that the rivalries with other singers got good press coverage. Her personal life, especially her marriages and the affair with Nicolini before their marriage, offered fine publicity potential.

Mapleson, we should observe, was a major force in spreading opera to cities beyond the East Coast. When he included Chicago in his first tour in the 1878-1879 season, he got an enthusiastic reception and stayed for two weeks, producing operas such as Le Nozze di Figaro and I puritani with a company that glittered with his London stars, Gerster, Hauk, Galassi, Del Puente and conductor Arditi. At that time, Chicago was much less important musically than Cincinnati and would remain so until the auditorium designed by Louis H. Sullivan and Dankmar Adler was opened in 1889. Then in the last decade of the century, Theodore Thomas arrived to create the symphony, and musically the city came of age. It had been, however, a stop for traveling opera companies since before the Civil War. Max Strakosch brought Amalia Patti to Chicago in the spring of 1866 in the Ghioni and Susini Grand Italian Opera Company (which went as far south as Columbus, Georgia), returning a month later to give L'Africaine. Other companies came with light or serious works but usually for only a few nights.

Going further afield, Mapleson arrived in San Francisco in the spring of 1884 to give that city its most artistically sophisticated dose of opera to date. There, operatic life had grown in importance in post Civil War years as traveling companies, such as the Richings English Opera Troupe, made their way west. In 1868 the Parepa-Rosa company arrived by steamship to present fifty nights of opera, and when the Union Pacific railroad was completed in next year various others, including a French comic opera company, Marie Aimée with her opéra-bouffe productions, the Alice Oates Company with Pinafore, and others could wend their way to the coast.[24]

GROWTH OF GERMAN OPERA

As German operas developed a following and seemed to promise a wider audience, many impresarios turned to producing them and translating other standard works into German. By 1878 even Maretzek, with his experience almost exclusively in Italian opera, was conducting J. C. Freyer's German Opera Company in St.Louis with Eugénie Pappenheim and Charles Adams in a repertory that included Lohengrin, Fidelio, Tannhäuser, The Flying Dutchman, and some non-German works. "Maretzek the Magnificent" had continued to manage opera companies until about 1874, after which he mainly conducted for other managers; according to Offenbach he was "an excellent orchestra leader."[25]

A growing competition between Italian and German opera had become, by the 1870s, a leitmotif for the seasonal rise and fall of impresarios and their performers. Although Armstrong in Philadelphia observed directly after the Civil War that German companies were generally weaker than Italian, the former improved as they moved into the hands of better trained musicians.[26] The same J. C. Freyer later to employ Maretzek had held a Wagner festival in New York in 1876 with Adolph Neuendorff conducting and the following year had taken a German company on a tour that included Cincinnati.

Cincinnati had become a major stop on the circuits of opera impresarios shortly after the Civil War and by 1870 was recognized as a major musical center in the Midwest. Its German population supported numerous musical institutions, including several choral societies, one orchestra, a Conservatory of Music and active operatic seasons carried on by traveling companies. These comprised a mixture of Italian, German, and English companies, with the added attraction of French opéra-bouffe, which soon shifted to Gilbert and Sullivan. During 1874 the city saw a little more than two weeks of Italian opera of which Aida was the big hit, about four weeks of opera in German by two companies (Louise Lichtmay's was one of the poorer ones), two weeks of Kellogg's English Opera Company, one week of Aimée's French Opéra-Bouffe Company and two weeks of the Oates Comic Opera Company (doing French opéra-bouffe in translation). Four years later there was a bit more than three weeks of Italian opera, three weeks of opera in English and about a week and a half of French opéra-bouffe.[27] In the early 1880s the College of Music of Cincinnati, whose first musical director had been Theodore Thomas, added an opera department with Max Maretzek as its head. More important, Maretzek helped prepare the first of Cincinnati's famous Opera Festivals that continued until 1884.

The selection of Maretzek for these two positions indicates his position in the operatic world. A benefit given for him at the Metropolitan Opera House eight years before he died in 1897 had the support and participation of the most prominent conductors (all German) then living in New York, including Walter Damrosch, Anton Seidl, Adolph Neuendorff and Theodore Thomas. Clearly Maretzek had been a crucial force in the production of opera for thirty years, bringing many of the finest singers and works to this country. Like the Strakosch brothers and Grau, he clung to the old Italian repertory and the old ideas, hoping that familiar tunes sung by new personalities would be enough to fill the theaters, and for a while they were.

The singers and conductors who performed German opera were not devoted exclusively to it, but turned to it for its fresher audience appeal, because German singers were appearing on the scene and also, doubtless, for its quality and the change of musical style. Louise Lichtmay had sung Elsa in Lohengrin under Neuendorff in New York, where she sang for several seasons in the 1870s.[28] She also took her Grand German Opera Company to Philadelphia in 1871 with singers Bertha Roemer, Theodore Habelmann, Carl Formes, and others. The repertory consisted of Fidelio, The Merry Wives of Windsor, Faust, Tannhäuser, Don Giovanni, Martha, Der Freischütz, The Jewess (Halévy), The Magic Flute, Alessandro Stradella (von Flotow), The Marriage of Figaro and Die weisse Dame (The White Lady).[29] Cincinnati, where

Lichtmay sang and consistently brought troupes, was especially receptive to the German works. Soprano Eugénie Pappenheim joined with Neuendorff to present some Wagnerian works in Boston in 1876 and tenor Theodor Wachtel also headed a German opera company at one point. Audiences, critics and musicians were ready for greater variety and new operas.

In the larger perspective German opera took a while to become established and had only sporadic performances during the 1860s and early 1870s, for time was needed to find more advocates for a German repertory, to train the necessary performers in it, and give it exposure to a broad audience. By the time conductor Carl Anschütz repeated *Tannhäuser* five years after Bergmann's first production in 1859, critics and audiences had heard a wider sampling of Wagner in orchestral concerts and were more receptive to the opera. Also, Anschütz had been busy staging other German works, *Der Freischütz*, *Die Zauberflöte*, and German translations of *Don Giovanni*, *Barber of Seville*, and *Faust* on circuits around New York.

Although Anschütz' soloists were judged inferior to those of the Italian troupes, the less familiar repertory he initiated was appreciated. He staged American premieres of Nicolai's *The Merry Wives of Windsor*, Spohr's *Jessonda*, and the first two acts of Gounod's *Mireille*, accompanied by the more familiar *Martha*, *Die weisse Dame* and others. In Boston in the mid-1860s Dwight gave high marks to a German company conducted by Anschütz, commenting on his "thorough musicianship, his mastery as a conductor, [and] that a most refreshing degree of unity, animation and artistic feeling has been realized in their performances."[30] Wagner's impact was increased when Anschütz' pupil Neuendorff directed a dozen presentations of *Lohengrin* (the performances with Lichtmay) in 1871 at New York's Stadt Theater. The presentation received a very positive reception, as the *Tribune* critic Hassard stated, "we must pronounce *Lohengrin* one of the most effective of modern lyric compositions."[31] Neuendorff then followed this, in collaboration with Freyer, with the above noted Wagner festival of 1876 that included American premieres of *The Flying Dutchman* and *Die Walküre* (*The Valkyrie*). By that time *Lohengrin* had made a successful debut in Italian at the Academy of Music, the

Italian opera stronghold, with internationally known stars Christine Nilsson and Italo Campanini.

Lohengrin (premiered in Weimar, in 1850) well illustrates the emerging characteristics of Wagner's music dramas. The composer wrote the libretto himself, as he always did, basing it on the legend of Lohengrin, the son of Parsifal (king of the Grail), whose mission is to help the falsely accused. Action takes place in tenth-century Antwerp near the river Scheldt where Elsa, the heroine, becomes the innocent victim of the ambitious Telramund and his wife, the sorceress Ortrud, who covet Elsa's dukedom. The swan that brings Lohengrin in his glittering armor to defend Elsa is actually her own brother bewitched by Ortrud. Here we have some basic Wagnerian ingredients of myth mixed with history, sorcery, and magic all stirred into a libretto whose purpose is the unique Wagnerian fusion of words, action and music, an interplay that is fundamental to his work. Later, in Der Ring des Nibelungen (The Ring of the Nibelung), his theories and philosophizing, at times long and dull, tended to get in the way of the drama. This very theorizing, however, was typical of the nineteenth century in northern Europe as was the genuine adulation for music as the highest of art forms. The later philosophizing was as fundamental to Wagner's large conceptions as his use of a mystical-religious world full of symbols.

Musically, Lohengrin to a great extent lacks the familiar division of recitative and aria found in Italian opera, so it is difficult to extract individual pieces for concert. The bridal music, however, attained a universal popularity which it maintains to this day. As time went on the composer's technique of "endless melody," stretching from beginning to end of a scene or act, was accompanied by a frequently modulating harmony to aid the melodic flow. This development of chromatic harmony, which reached its apex in Tristan, was as striking a departure from past operatic practice as his lengthy drawing out of the melodic line with its interwoven leitmotifs. The orchestra was expanded to symphonic proportions as it took on an essential role that, like an on-going commentary, paralleled, enlarged and developed the stage action. Leitmotifs played by the orchestra were identified with a character (or a character's thought or feeling), an object, or an idea and singly, or in combinations, created another level of continuing expression that Wagner called the "inner aspect" of the drama. An imaginative orchestral innovator, Wagner's music exemplifies the general nineteenth-century trend toward greater sonority and range of color in orchestration.

GERMAN MUSICAL INFLUENCE

To be clear about the emergence of German influences on musicians in general it is necessary to look back and digress briefly. German musical taste and activity had been apparent since the arrival of the German-speaking Moravians in Pennsylvania in the eighteenth century. Music, much of it by German composers, was an integral part of their life but because of their clannish habits, little of their musical sophistication and skill spilled over into the surrounding society. It was not until late in 1848 that a highly visible group of German musicians arrived to focus attention strongly on the works of German masters such as Haydn, Mozart, Beethoven, and Mendelssohn. This, the thoroughly trained Germania Orchestra, was composed of instrumentalists who had been formerly employed in Berlin in the orchestras of the nobility. Besides symphonic works, they played the opera overtures of Donizetti, Weber, Meyerbeer and Adam and gave concerts with singers such as opera divas Fortunata Tedesco and Rosa Devries. Although the Germania disbanded in 1854 its effect was long lasting, for its members settled in larger cities mainly in the Northeast and in Chicago to pass on their skills and repertory through performances and teaching. This was the beginning of a German line of strongly influential conductors that included Carl Bergmann, Carl Anschütz, Adolph Neuendorff, Theodore Thomas and Leopold and Walter Damrosch.

With the dissolution of the Germania Orchestra, the group's former conductor, Carl Bergmann, became conductor of the Arion Society in New York, in 1855 alternate conductor of the New York Philharmonic Society, and for a while of the Brooklyn Philharmonic Society. Carl Zerrahn, one of the Germania's flutists, took over as conductor of the Handel and Haydn Society and the

Harvard Symphony concerts in Boston. Some Germania members may also have assumed positions at the newly developing music schools and conservatories of the late 1860s. While Peabody had been established in Baltimore in 1857, a decade elapsed before the founding of the New England Conservatory and Boston Conservatory, both in Boston and the Conservatory in Cincinnati. Many of the instrumentalists doubtless had private pupils to whom they passed on their techniques, musicianship, and taste. A telling measure of the influence of the Germania's seven hundred or more concerts, their excellence and repertory is in the large number of groups assuming the same name that arose in the next decades.[32]

Bergmann, as conductor of several major musical groups in New York and as an advocate of the German music of Schumann, Beethoven and the "new" German music of Wagner, and Liszt, had an enormous influence on the taste of his audiences. It was Bergmann who directed and, with the aid of the Arion Society, staged the first performance in America of Wagner's Tannhäuser on April 4, 1859, at the Stadt Theater in New York. The New York Herald reported that "the music is quite of the new school, and elicited the most marked approval from a very critical audience. The opera [had] . . . a fine orchestra, and scenery, . . . with good artists." William Henry Fry, critic at the Tribune, whose tastes ran to Italian rather than German opera, was less enthusiastic.

We have noted performances of Der Freischütz, in many forms, since the 1820s and the popularity of von Flotow's Martha, which became a favorite role for many sopranos. Even the ever popular La Dame blanche had been transformed into Die weisse Dame. Other works by German composers, as well as German plays, however, appeared to be directed toward the entertainment of the German-speaking community of New York, which wished to preserve German art and culture, rather than the mainstream of theatrical entertainment. Bergmann, who spent the first twenty-eight years of his life studying and performing in Germany, had thoroughly absorbed the German repertory and style and believed that German music was of a superior type.[33] As a supporter of contemporary works, he would leave his impression more on orchestral music than opera, but his introduction of a complete Wagnerian piece was of crucial importance.

Tannhäuser revealed a different conception of musical and dramatic style from Italian opera and a different kind of artistic beauty. Wagner's approach to the stage, his orchestral and vocal techniques, and his brand of mid-century romanticism from northern Europe contrasted sharply with that of Verdi and the earlier Italians. Because it was new, it met with mixed responses but appealed strongly to the German population. Wagner's real impact on opera in this country would come only after the building of the Metropolitan Opera House in New York.

A strong catalyst for German music and indirectly for Wagnerian opera was conductor Theodore Thomas (1835-1905). This admirer of Wagner, born in Germany in 1835, became probably the most important influence on musical taste in America after the Civil War. A fine violinist, Thomas had played with the Germania Orchestra when it accompanied Jenny Lind and other opera singers in concerts and became a member of the chamber group, along with Carl Bergmann, that William Mason formed to give the first consistent and successful chamber music series in New York. He made his debut as an opera conductor in 1859 when he replaced Anschütz for a performance of Lucrezia Borgia. Before the end of the Civil War Thomas had his own orchestra and was hard at work offering audiences a first class, primarily German, instrumental repertory. In fact he saw himself as a man with a mission, namely to educate listeners by bringing them the best music he knew. He lured his audiences in by mixing lighter, popular fare with the more serious and by giving first class performances. Many commented on the truly excellent quality of his orchestra. Anton Rubinstein, founder of the St. Petersburg Conservatory and a giant among the pianists of his generation, on the completion of an American tour with the Thomas Orchestra in 1873 stated that hardly any European orchestra could compare with that of Thomas.[34] Other musicians echoed that evaluation. Thomas did not confine his efforts to New York City, but took his orchestra repeatedly on lengthy tours of what became known as the "Thomas Highway," which followed the railroad lines through the northeast to Chicago and returned via St. Louis, Louisville, and Baltimore.

The attitude and devotion to "serious" German music by

Bergmann, Thomas, Leopold Damrosch, and others during the 1860s and '70s had other effects on the audience besides educating them. "Serious" musicians became identified with German music, not Italian or French, and their music was increasingly viewed as special, a means of edification or of raising the individual to a higher, more spiritual level. Music (German), therefore, was not simply for one's enjoyment, but also for one's improvement. This semi-religious aura further implied that it was not for everyone, but rather the select few who "understood" it and were in sympathy with its "mission." And if you were "in the know," you should not have to ask how to understand it or what the mission was. In Philharmonic: History of New York's Orchestra, Howard Shanet expressed it clearly:

> These self-righteous attitudes were shared by a small but determined part of the listening public, who sometimes seemed to constitute a semi-religious congregation; by a large number of performing musicians who functioned as artists-priests; and by certain composers, who, if we carry our figure a bit further, seem inescapably to have aspired toward some degree of divinity.[35]

This was the same sentiment that Wagner himself promoted and succeeded in inculcating in his audiences in Germany. It would later help promote his operas here.

THE AMERICAN COMPOSER

American composers drawn to opera in the nineteenth century encountered not only the complexities, questions, and obstacles inherent in the genre itself, but also those of creating music that had an American sound or a national idiom. William Fry, who, in articles and lectures, argued for an American national style, himself turned to Italian models for his Leonora, the text of which was based on an English author's drama in a French setting.[36] Although originally written and sung in English at its 1845 premiere, Leonora was translated into Italian when it moved to New York's Academy of Music in 1858. George Frederick

Bristow chose an American subject for his Rip Van Winkle (1855), but, like Fry, drew on European musical style. In the mid-1850s virtuoso violinist Ole Bull offered a $1,000 prize for an American opera, but the contest floundered before it could elicit a response. Max Maretzek used an American subject in his opera Sleepy Hollow; or, The Headless Horseman (New York, 1879), which again followed Italian models. Dudley Buck's Deseret; or, A Saint's Affliction, a work on the Mormons and their practice of polygamy, was considered too religious musically, and went unpublished, as did a number of other operas by Americans of that time.[37] The isolation and alienation of the American composer grew as opera became increasingly viewed as a European entertainment to be enjoyed by a wealthy aristocracy similar to that of the old world with little to offer the new. Even the operatic language, English up to the Civil War, had shifted to Italian in the second half of the century because of the repertory, managers, singers and the complexity of social factors.

Composers sought superior musical training in Europe, especially Germany, although a number of conservatories (such as Peabody Institute in Baltimore, New England Conservatory, Cincinnati Conservatory, Chicago Musical College) had been established here. In Germany one learned German style and technique and a reverence for the masterworks of German music. Americans in general were viewed as inferiors by many and this view doubtless extended to the artist and any artistic creation. A similar position until very recently has been assigned to women.

In the same vein, European impresarios and singers were determined to keep opera within their own province and opposed the approach of any American. Minnie Hauk noted how strongly the German company resented her when she was singing with them in New York. Nancy Storace had received the same treatment by singers of the Italian Opera Company in London in the late eighteenth century. Protecting one's territory was an old story. The legend that Americans were incapable of performing or producing fine music was an accepted one and one that Europeans promulgated for their own advantage. America had, in fact, produced fine performers in Minnie Hauk, Clara Louise Kellogg and David Bispham, to name only the best known. Regarding the composition of opera, critics were on fairly safe ground if they were comparing the few known works by Americans with the body of European work that came from long established musical traditions. Despite this arid picture, in which the second half of the nineteenth century was a desert for the American composer, a background of knowledge, practice, standards, and taste was developing. When Americans finally started seeking training in their own institutions in the next century, innate creativity began to come into its own, other attitudes arose, and possibilities began to present themselves.

CONCLUSION

Opera in English traveled two paths after the Civil War. The first consisted of translated European works mixed with those of English composers such as Balfe, Wallace and others, while the second comprised the operettas of Gilbert and Sullivan. The latter were characterized by a comic spirit laced with satire and a fresh style of joining words and music.

In France, Germany, and later Italy, new approaches to both subjects and music had developed. A pattern in the more general history of European music that music historians categorize as "exotic" appeared most strikingly in France. Carmen was one of a group of works going back to Meyerbeer's L'Africaine of 1865 that focused on this type of subject matter. Delibes' Lakmé, Saint-Saëns's Samson et Dalila, and Bizet's Les Pêcheurs de perles (The Pearl Fishers) joined the group by the last decade of the century. In Carmen Seville and Spanish mountains form the foreign setting, enhanced by Bizet's use of some Spanish folk melodies as in the "Entr'acte" preceding Act IV. Gaza in ancient Israel is Samson et Dalila's setting, for which Saint-Saëns suggests Middle Eastern chant and the drones common to Middle Eastern music. Aida follows the same trend in Italian opera. It takes place in Egypt's royal city of Memphis with a temple and the banks of the Nile forming further background that Verdi colors by special orchestral effects to lend an Eastern flavor to parts of the music. Carmen, Selika (L'Africaine) and Lakmé are all loved by or enamored with military or naval European men of a higher social cast. The "exotic" or "foreign" aspect of the women is in part what makes them desirable to these more conventional if aggressive males and also probably to their audience.

Wagner brought an original vision to his music dramas, in which he created a new style of singing and for which he himself wrote the librettos based on myths. Musically, the changes effected by his expanded orchestration, widening harmonic language and new views of thematic material were powerful. Whether it is Wagner's huge symphonic orchestra or Bizet's coloristic use of castanets, the result was far different from the dominating strings of Rossini or Bellini.

German musicians who came to these shores brought a narrow, chauvinistic view to the American scene, but also they slowly and steadily raised musical standards. By the time Theodore Eisfeld became the first of the long line of German conductors of the New York Philharmonic in 1852, three-quarters of the instrumentalists were German.[38] Their influence on American musical life was powerful. Better trained than most of their Italian, British, or American colleagues, they introduced much higher levels of technical proficiency into both the symphonic and opera orchestras in which they played, while always promoting German music as the highest art.

NOTES

1. Jacques Offenbach, Orpheus in America: Offenbach's Diary of his Journey to the New World, trans. Lander MacClintock (Bloomington: Indiana University Press, 1957), p. 70.
2. J. C. Furnas, The Americans: A Social History of the United States, 1587-1914 (Toronto: Longmans, 1969), p. 613.
3. Edward Ellsworth Hipsher, American Opera and Its Composers: A Complete History of Serious American Opera, with a Summary of the Lighter Forms Which Led Up to Its Birth, 2nd ed. (Philadelphia: Theodore Presser Co., 1934), p. 37.

4. Larry Robert Wolz, "Opera in Cincinnati before 1920: The Years Before the Zoo, 1801-1920," (Ph.D. dissertation, University of Cincinnati, 1983), p. 246.

5. Michael Turner, ed., The Parlour Song Book, A Casquet of Vocal Gems (New York: Viking Press, 1972), p. 216.

6. Clara Louise Kellogg, Memoirs of an American Prima Donna (New York: G. P. Putnam's Sons, The Knickerbocker Press, 1913), p. 256.

7. Ibid., p. 56.

8. Leslie Baily, Gilbert and Sullivan and Their World (London: Thames and Hudson, 1973), p. 52.

9. The Boston Ideal Opera Company, which staged Pinafore, grew out of the Boston Theater Company and became an important group staging light opera and operettas.

10. W. G. Armstrong, Record of the Opera in Philadelphia (New York: AMS Press, 1976), p. 150.

11. Wolz, Opera in Cincinnati, p. 244.

12. Deane L. Root, American Popular Stage Music 1860-1880 (Ann Arbor, MI: UMI Research Press, 1981), p. 116. Chapter 4 gives detailed information on European operettas of this period.

13. Donald Jay Grout with Hermine Weigel Williams, A Short History of Opera, 3rd ed. (New York: Columbia University Press, 1988), pp. 375-376.

14. David Cairns, ed. and trans., The Memoirs of Hector Berlioz (New York: W. W. Norton & Co., Inc., 1975), pp. 324-325.

15. Luigi Arditi, My Reminiscences (New York: Dodd Mead, 1896), p. 282.

16. Armstrong, Record of the Opera in Philadelphia, p. 208.

17. Minnie Hauk, Memories of a Singer (New York: Arno Press, reprint, 1977), p. 47.

18. John Frederick Cone, First Rival of The Metropolitan Opera (New York: Columbia University Press, 1983), p. 157.

19. Dwight's Journal of Music, November 23, 1878.

20. Winton Dean, George Bizet: His Life and Work (London: J. Dent and Sons Ltd., 1965), p. 119.

21. Harold Rosenthal, ed., The Mapleson Memoirs: The Career of an Operatic Impresario 1858-1888 (New York: Appleton-Century, 1966), p. 152.

22. Cone, First Rival, p. 43.

23. Ibid., p. 44.

24. Cornel Lengyel, ed., Music of the Gold Rush Era (New York: AMS Press Reprint, 1972), vols. 4 & 7.

25. Offenbach, Orpheus in America, p. 123.

26. Armstrong, Record of the Opera in Philadelphia, p. 127.

27. Wolz, "Opera in Cincinnati," pp. 247-248; 250-251.

28. Esther Singleton, "History of the Opera in New York from 1750 to 1898," The Musical Courier, 23, (1898).

29. Armstrong, Record of the Opera in Philadelphia, p. 162.

30. Dwight's Journal of Music, May 14, 1864.

31. Mark McKnight, "Wagner and the New York Press, 1855-76," American Music V (1987), p. 149.

32. H. Earle Johnson, "The Germania Musical Society," Musical Quarterly XXXIX/1 (1953), p. 92.

33. Ibid., p. 75.

34. Ezra Schabas, Theodore Thomas: America's Conductor and Builder of Orchestras, 1835-1905 (Chicago: University of Illinois Press, 1989), p. 52.

35. Howard Shanet, Philharmonic: A History of New York's Orchestra (New York: Doubleday, 1975), p. 144.

36. See Vera B. Lawrence, "William Henry Fry's Messianic Yearnings," American Music 7 (1989): 382-411.

37. H. Earle Johnson, Operas on American Subjects (New York: Coleman-Ross, Co., 1964), p. 37.

38. Shanet, Philharmonic, p. 109.

6

A Turn to German Opera: 1883–1900

> Meanwhile, however, Wagner, to show what he meant, abandoned operatic composition altogether, and took to writing dramatic poems, and using all the resources of the orchestral harmony and vocal tone to give them the utmost reality and intensity of expression, thereby producing the new art form which he called "music drama," which is no more "reformed opera" than a cathedral is a reformed stone quarry.
>
> George Bernard Shaw
> from The Tone Poet

The term "Gilded Age," borrowed from Mark Twain's satire The Gilded Age (1873), elicits scattered memories of radically contradictory images. Obvious examples are the enormous untaxed wealth of a few contrasted with the pittance paid a factory worker for a fourteen-hour day; the completion of the Union Pacific railroad west and the final bloody battles with Indians; women protected by rich velvet gowns in Victorian mansions and others battling for individual recognition and the vote. This was the era of the "robber barons" and the completion of western expansion as well as the less immediately spectacular, if more lasting, inventions of the incandescent light bulb, the telegraph, telephone, and phonograph. A general political mediocrity, social ostentation, and ruthless commercialism characterized the times, coupled with suspicion and intolerance of political dissidents and unions and intense discrimination against minority groups. All was overcast with the shadow of Victorian prudery.

Lack of political leadership elicited the comment from historian Henry Adams that "One might search the whole list of Congress, Judiciary, and Executive during the twenty-five years of 1870-1895 and find little but damaged reputations."[1] Such a political climate, so unlike the early part of the century, permitted unchecked commercial speculation, which in turn produced extraordinary fortunes. The riches of a Morgan or a Vanderbilt are now difficult to imagine, but if one visits the Morgan Library in New York, housed in part of the financial tycoon's home, one sees a type of opulence approaching that of European royalty.

The Vanderbilt family was the moving spirit behind the construction of the Metropolitan Opera House, which they and a few other families, including the Roosevelts and Morgans, easily financed. This group, which had made its fortunes during or following the Civil War, was unacceptable to New York's established social leaders, who had been wealthy from the time of the Revolution. Hence, the nouveau-riche were refused boxes at the Academy of Music, a symbol of approved acceptance, and here lay the problem. Old money was not interested in sitting next to new money even in a box at the opera, and so the Metropolitan was built. There the newcomers had their own theater, which supplied the desired evenings of socializing with the "right" people in a setting of cultural uplift. As had been the case with the Astor Place Opera House thirty-five years before, the design of the Metropolitan aimed for broad visibility among members of the audience and only secondarily a view of the stage. Little attention was paid or space allotted to the backstage area in which all of the machinery, sets, costumes, dressing rooms and other paraphernalia for performances had to be housed.

The rich supporters of the Metropolitan had donned the expensive cloak of European opera to advertise their special position and wealth, just as the shareholders of the old Academy of Music had done before them. After all, Patti got $5,000 a performance, and anything that cost that much must be the best. Besides, she was famous in Europe and sang European works.

THE MUSICAL SCENE

The closing decades of the century presented several operatic features that distinguish them from the past. A permanent home for opera, the Metropolitan, was built; German opera came into its own; singers in Italian troupes now played almost exclusively to a rich audience and demanded huge fees, often endangering a company's financial status; and a major effort was undertaken to popularize opera in English and accompany it with the creation of a National Conservatory of Music to train American singers.

Although the motivation behind the construction of the Metropolitan Opera House had less to do with music than with money and social hierarchy, the new building would eventually stabilize New York's operatic life. In the new theater German works found a consistent home in the repertory with high standards of musical and vocal artistry nurtured by conductors Leopold Damrosch and Anton Seidl and singers such as Lilli Lehmann, Marianne Brandt, and Max Alvary. Damrosch (1832-1885), a fine violinist who had toured in Europe with pianists Hans von Bülow and Carl Tausig, immigrated to New York to conduct the Arion Society, one of the city's older, established choral groups. Seidl (1850-1898) at thirty-five was one of Wagner's favored inner circle and had worked closely with him to prepare performances at the festival theater that had been built specifically for Wagnerian works at Bayreuth. Lehmann (1848-1929), whose extraordinary talent, industry, and critical powers placed her in the first rank of singers, had sung under Wagner in some of the premieres of his works. On the Italian side, the repertory was older, singers higher paid, and performances less concerned with the total effect of the ensemble than with the star. Adelina Patti had a pet parrot who imitated her whistle as well as some of her English and French phrases and, according to Mapleson, would cry "cash, cash" whenever he entered her car on the touring train.[2]

Opera in English became a major project undertaken by wealthy music-lover Jeannette Thurber, whose aim was its popularization. She envisioned separate opera companies in major cities that would be attached to conservatories which in turn would train American singers. To this end she hired Theodore Thomas as conductor of her opera company that through touring would introduce and initiate her proposals.

ACADEMY OF MUSIC VERSUS METROPOLITAN

The Academy of Music had been home to New York's wealthiest patrician families since it opened in 1854 with Norma. There, the Astors, Schuylers, Belmonts and such could attend, assured of hearing a familiar repertory and seeing friends or relatives in their familiar boxes emblazoned with names of famous singers of the past. For these families the Academy was an important and guarded symbol of New York's inner circle for whom Mapleson had been staging opera as a regular part of his tours since 1878. He saw the opening of the Metropolitan as a clear threat to his supremacy and one that must be met head on. His experience, ability and public relations tactics were effective and formidable. Vanderbilts, Morgans, Whitneys, and their set, the shareholders of the new opera house, securely settled in their own boxes, hired Henry Abbey as their manager, despite the fact that his experience was in the legitimate theater rather than the opera house. The spring before the Metropolitan opened, Mapleson and soprano Christine Nilsson had a lengthy and acrimonious feud in the papers, cleverly initiated by the former, which effectively advertised both companies. Nilsson would inaugurate the Metropolitan but had previously been under contract to Mapleson. He strongly implied that she was past her prime, her voice virtually gone, and that there were few roles left that she could sing. She heatedly replied that he did not know what he was talking about, and back an forth it went.[3] Mapleson also claimed that Abbey was trying to steal his singers, which produced more newspaper columns. Meantime, Patti added to the publicity by playing both managers against each other whenever possible for her own financial benefit.

The rival companies opened on the same night, October 22, 1883, and subsequent performances were also scheduled for the same evenings. Darwin's theory of the survival of the fittest, then especially popular with the successful, was to be played out. At the Academy the famous Hungarian soprano Etelka Gerster, greatly admired by critic Richard Grant White, sang in La sonnambula with tenor Eugenio Vicini in his American debut under veteran conductor Arditi to a sold-out house and an enthusiastic reception. At the Metropolitan, Faust (in Italian) with Christine Nilsson and Italo Campanini, who had come out of retirement for this season, began late and was equally criticized as well as acclaimed.[4] The choices of Bellini's opera, fifty-two years old, and Gounod's, twenty-four years old, both of which had been performed innumerable times in English and Italian, could hardly have been safer or more conservative.

Each company's repertory included nine works of long standing, the so-called "old favorites." A total of twenty other operas, ten given under each impresario, were either revivals of older works, such as Rossini's La gazza ladra, which Patti had done with success in the previous London season, or newer ones such as Ponchielli's La Gioconda ("The Joyful Girl"), also well received in the preceding London season (see Table I). Abbey's wonderful staging of Gioconda brought out a large, enthusiastic audience that "afforded convincing proof of the eagerness for a change from the stale list which had so long constituted its operatic pabulum."[5] In fact, the repertory of the companies, aside from the shared works, was quite varied, and the rosters of singers shone with the most famous stars of the day. Besides those mentioned, Lillian Nordica, tenor Ernest Nicolini (Patti's husband), and baritone Antonio Galassi sang for Mapleson, while Marcella Sembrich, contralto Sofia Scalchi and baritone Giuseppe Del Puente sang for Abbey at the Metropolitan.

Despite their stars, "popular" repertories and tours, both managers lost money, the operatically naive Abbey more than the resilient Mapleson. The orchestra at the Metropolitan was less skilled, the acoustics poor, the sight lines unsatisfactory, intermissions long because of inadequate backstage facilities, and the architecture described as ordinary. Originally the orchestra was to be sunk below the stage level to improve the view of the singers and acoustics, but conductor Vianesi did not approve this arrangement so the orchestra was elevated to its accustomed, if

TABLE 1
Academy versus Metropolitan Repertory, 1883-1884 Season

The Shared Repertory:

La sonnambula
I puritani
La traviata
Les Huguenots
Il trovatore
Rigoletto
Lucia di Lammermoor
Faust
Martha

****

Individual Repertory:

Academy:	Metropolitan:
Linda di Chamounix	The Barber of Seville
La gazza ladra	Don Giovanni
La favorite	La Gioconda
Norma	Lohengrin
Ernani	Robert le Diable
Aida	Carmen
L'elisir d'amore	Mefistofele
Crispino e la comare	Hamlet
Semiramide	Mignon
Roméo et Juliette	Le Prophète

obstructive position.[6] Most important, the financial losses were staggering. By the middle of November Abbey was losing about $15,000, a week, which would mount to a total of about $600,000 by the end of the season, including a tour; this deficit would lead to his resignation.[7] New York could not sustain two competing companies performing Italian opera. It was time for a change of more than just the manager.

CONVERSION TO A GERMAN REPERTORY

Negotiations by the Metropolitan's directors with Ernest Gye, manager at Covent Garden, to take over the Metropolitan had failed by summer, and the prospect of a fall season seemed unlikely. At this point Leopold Damrosch came forward with a proposal that was musically innovative and, more important to the directors, appeared financially sound. Damrosch saw the time as propitious for changing from the threadbare past repertory to the new one coming to life in Europe, specifically in Germany. He knew that Wagner's works were uniquely different from other opera, probably would attract the musically aware German speaking population in New York that had some familiarity with German opera anyway, and might, because they were viewed as progressive, appeal to the socially elite. Damrosch proposed that he would conduct and produce German operas and works translated into German at reduced ticket prices (down from $7 to $4), which would be possible by hiring German singers, who were considerably less expensive than the Italian. The ensemble would be the focus rather than the star. Damrosch would use the New York Symphony, an excellent group which he had formed some time before, as the orchestra and when needed supplement the German chorus with members of his Oratorio Society. It was a comprehensive, well reasoned offer and the directors hired him. During this "Wagnerian High Tide," as critic Henry Krehbiel called it, the consistently fine quality of the totality of these performances would inevitably raise audience sophistication and expectation.[8]

Damrosch, a friend of Liszt under whom he had played at Weimar, had left Breslau in 1871 for the wider opportunities of

New York to become the new conductor of the Arion Society and shortly to form the Oratorio Society and the Symphony Society. A first-class violinist who had studied and practiced medicine to please his parents before he turned to his first love, music, Leopold was a thoroughly trained musician and conductor with the beginnings of a solid European reputation when he arrived here. Married to a fine singer who had also worked under Liszt, their household which numbered five children was immersed in music. Ultimately the Damrosch family, especially Walter, Frank and Clara (who married David Mannes) would have a far reaching effect on American musical taste and education.[9]

Leopold promptly went to Europe to secure the singers and stage personnel for the new Metropolitan season. Through his German contacts and offers of good salaries he was able to hire some excellent, dedicated singers who had worked with Wagner at Bayreuth on the Ring des Nibelungen cycle. The most famous among them was Amalia Materna, who had appeared in the first performances of Siegfried and Götterdämmerung (Twilight of the Gods) in 1876 and was known here for her appearances in concert under Theodore Thomas in New York six years later.

The repertory of this first season of German opera ranged from Wagner's Tannhäuser and Die Walküre to German translations of Don Giovanni and Rigoletto. Least successful were Fidelio and Der Freischütz, probably because of their spoken dialogue, which tended to become lost in the large theater and to which only some of the audience could respond. Another casualty was Don Giovanni which suffered from poor staging and translation.[10] The Wagnerian works, including Lohengrin and Meyerbeer's Le Prophète, received high marks. Krehbiel also notes that the size of the Metropolitan encouraged the grand gestures of Meyerbeer and the dramatic, declamatory style of Wagner rather than the lightness of comedy or more intimate types of work. Despite the problems, the new course of less expensive tickets and singers and new repertory proved sound as the box office profits increased. Apparently the new German segment of the audience that Damrosch had hoped for was beginning to appear.

The crowning achievement of the season was Die Walküre,

which was staged essentially as it had been done at Bayreuth where Damrosch had seen it when the cycle was first done as a whole under Wagner's direction. Scenery, costumes and stage direction were copied as closely as possible and as was practical. Three of the female singers, Materna, Kraus (later to marry the Metropolitan's future conductor, Anton Seidl), and Brandt had sung under Wagner and so brought invaluable knowledge to rehearsals and performance. Damrosch scheduled enough rehearsals to ensure the security of the singers in their roles, the orchestra in its part, and the accomplishment of the fusion of words, drama, and music. Significantly, some of the music was already familiar through excerpts, notably the "Ride of the Valkyries" that had been done in concert. The fine ensemble work of the German singers and Brandt's gripping performance as Brünnhilde succeeded so well that the work was repeated seven times in the remainder of the season.

In order to implement his ideas for his music dramas (a term he preferred to "opera"), Wagner wrote his own librettos, shaping language and poetry as he saw fit. He could also take advantage of his vast knowledge of stagecraft and acting to create scenes and mold characters. As he turned to myth and legend for subjects, he drew on universal threads and what Freud would later call "the unconscious." A prolific writer on many subjects, Wagner set forth his theoretical and philosophical ideas on the direction of opera in the essay, *Oper und Drama*, published in 1852. Many of these concepts had already found expression in *Lohengrin*, but he carried them out more completely in *The Ring*, which he had started by 1850 with the poem of *Siegfrieds Tod* (*Siegfried's Death*). Believing that this drama, which was retitled to become *Die Götterdämmerung*, the last of the group, needed more background information, he worked backward to write the three preceding librettos (in order, *Das Rheingold* (*The Rhinegold*), *Die Walküre*, and *Siegfried*) and then worked from the beginning of this vast tetralogy to compose the music.

In *Die Walküre* Wagner modeled the poetic style of his libretto on that of medieval German verse to develop a distinctive sound. The drama looks back to Germanic myth for the many gods, demigods, and the other fantastic creatures it brings to life.

Struggles concerning the human traits of greed, jealousy, love, and infidelity are acted out in a grand, complex panorama that contains other supernatural objects (the magic sword for example) that are properties of the gods. Considering these ingredients, the allegorical possibilities and interpretations are varied, which is one of the compelling reasons why the Ring has remained fascinating to so many.

The music has almost no arias as such and little ensemble singing, for the vocal parts are in a declamatory style and the consistent word repetition of the older aria is absent. At intense dramatic moments, however, Wagner brings more lyrical elements effectively into play. This is not to say that melodic interest is lacking, for it is everywhere in the leitmotifs.

Unfortunately, Leopold Damrosch died a week before the end of this opera season he had shaped and which was so far-reaching in its importance. His son Walter, just twenty-three, conducted the remaining performances and the tour to Chicago, Cincinnati, and Boston that had been scheduled. At the close of the tour the directors sent Walter to Europe with instructions to hire the conductor and singers for the next season. He returned with conductor Anton Seidl, soprano Lilli Lehmann, tenor Max Alvary, and bass Emil Fischer. It was the beginning of a great Wagnerian period in America.

GERMAN REPERTORY AND PERFORMERS

The period from the 1884-1885 season through that of 1890-1891 consisted mainly of Wagner, supplemented with works by a few other German composers, most importantly Beethoven and Weber, and translations of standard works. Each season, besides the repetition of the more familiar Lohengrin and Tannhäuser, a Wagnerian premiere was presented: Die Meistersinger von Nürenberg (The Mastersingers of Nuremberg) and Tristan und Isolde (January and December respectively of 1886), Siegfried (1887), Das Rheingold and Die Götterdämmerung the next year (the latter in a cut version), and in the spring of 1889 The Ring was given as a whole. There were also works by lesser-known German composers such as Karl Goldmark (Die Königin von Saba, (The Queen of Sheba) and Peter Cornelius. Other works by some of their contemporaries are best forgotten. German translations concentrated on the more familiar Carmen, Faust, Rigoletto, and works of Meyerbeer. Damrosch's first season had set the tone with his carefully prepared Die Walküre, sung by an impressive company, some of whom would continue, with new additions, under Seidl.

Anton Seidl brought to New York an unusual level of musical standards and commitment. His extensive operatic experience, despite his youth, had included that of chorus master at the Vienna Opera, the post of assistant conductor at the first Bayreuth Festival under Wagner, eight years as conductor at the Municipal Theater in Leipzig, with which company he gave performances of The Ring in cities throughout Europe, and two years as conductor at the Municipal Theater in Bremen. He had assisted in preparing copies of scores for the Bayreuth Festival while he lived in the Wagner household and was a member of that inner circle. Recognized as one of the best young conductors in Europe, he had the word directly from the master. Like the singers who came with him, he saw the spread of Wagner's works as a sacred mission in which the totality of the work was greater than any of its parts, and that included the performers. The attitude toward Wagner's music is summed up by Lilli Lehmann: "Seidl, . . . Emil Fischer, . . . Alvary . . . were with us united, in loving comprehension and glowing adoration, to do homage to the majesty of the Master."[11]

Correspondence attests to the close friendship that existed between Lehmann, her mother, her two sisters and the Wagner family. Lilli and her sister Marie were in the first performances of The Ring at Bayreuth in lesser parts. A singer of unflagging determination and the highest standards and goals, Lehmann sang a huge number of roles during her career, in London, Berlin, Vienna and New York, that ranged from Lucia, in her earlier days, to Carmen, Isolde and Brünnhilde. She and Seidl were an extraordinary team that concentrated on the unity of the works, leaving no detail untouched and thus achieving excellent levels of performance as they introduced this new type of opera. Other singers who had worked with Wagner and/or had extensive experience in Germany, besides Lehmann, were Albert Niemann, a great singer nearing the end of his career who, according to Lehmann, "died as we never yet had seen Siegfried die," Emil Fischer, almost as popular as Lehmann and famous for his Sachs in Meistersinger, and a host of others.

An important factor in the success of the German repertory was Seidl's demand for a well-integrated ensemble that consisted of first-class singers. He required everyone to attend rehearsals and sing their parts throughout. When Max Alvary refused to sing at the rehearsal for the American premiere of Siegfried because he said it would strain his voice for the next night's performance, Seidl insisted that conductor and singers must hear him to work with him, and forced the issue by calling the head of the stockholders to his aid. Alvary sang the rehearsal and the performance. At rehearsals of the same opera Lehmann, in her enthusiasm for the success of the work, called on her Bayreuth experience to help rearrange some scenery to be closer to Bayreuth's staging and achieve better effects.[12]

The contrast with some attitudes and practices of the Italian companies is clear. Patti rarely attended rehearsals, sometimes meeting the cast for the first time on stage in the performance. She was unquestionably a great singer but saw herself as the main attraction rather than the opera. Kellogg complained, as did many others, of poorly prepared Italian chorus singers. Mapleson tended to schedule performances, except for the opening, only a few days ahead and had periodic cancellations often because of an ailing or temperamental singer. Although a solid musician, astute businessman and eternal optimist, Mapleson almost always lost money, owed everyone (except Patti), and more than once approached bankruptcy. In fact, it was very difficult for the usual traveling company to achieve predictable performance or financial consistency because of extra touring expenses, constant shifting to new theaters, and the physical and emotional stress of the travel itself. Under Seidl's strong leadership in one opera house, however, irregularities were few as performance stability developed along with a stronger financial base.

Another important reason for the success of the new

repertory was the positive response that appeared in the reviews of Henry Krehbiel (1854-1923) and W. J. Henderson (1855-1937), both knowledgeable and sympathetic critics. Of the two critics, William James Henderson, born in Newark, New Jersey, was perhaps the better trained musically and more creative as a writer. He authored the libretto for Walter Damrosch's second opera, Cyrano de Bergerac (1913), wrote a novel and a number of books on music, and was critic at The Times from 1887 until 1902. It was Krehbiel, however, who has left us specific chronicles of opera seasons in New York.

Henry Krehbiel had come to the musically influential New York Tribune from Cincinnati in 1880. Well regarded for his intelligence and scholarship by his colleagues, Krehbiel was an ardent supporter of Wagner. At the first New York performance of Tristan und Isolde, Krehbiel wrote a series of three long articles on its history and music. The weight of his opinions were doubtless a factor in the opera's success. Besides his reviews he lectured on music, wrote program notes for important New York concerts, and made a revised edition of Thayer's Life of Beethoven. While initially he welcomed new music, as time progressed he became less receptive to new ideas and rather rigid in his conservativism.

Wagner had interrupted his work on The Ring, which he began to think might never be performed, to create Tristan, which was premiered in Munich in 1865. In this less massive, more manageable project, the medieval myth he chose was well known to his audience, for it had served several poets, among them Tennyson. Wagner focused on only a few of the events in the legend to concentrate his opera into a compelling love story and one that incidentally coincided with his own love affair, perhaps more spiritual than physical, with Mathilde Wesendonck, wife of one of his benefactors. Audiences found this tragic tale of love that ends in death comprehensible as a drama, if unusual and intense. Little outward action takes place, and there are few of the scenic possibilities of the operas of The Ring, in which Rheinmaidens swim under water, Brünnhilde is surrounded by a ring of fire, a dragon appears, Valhalla goes up in flames and like, if lesser, events. In Tristan everything focuses on the inner feelings of the two main characters, their developing passion, and the inevitability of their fate.

The music, with its array of leitmotifs, is some of the most beautiful, tumultuous, and exciting that the composer ever wrote. Here one is in a complex, ever moving sea of harmony that is often ambiguous as to the main key or its harmonic direction. Melodic motion is often by semi-tones, and endings normally signified by cadences frequently merge with a continuing idea. From the start the work is one long, continuous arch of sound that only ends, despite the separation into acts, as Isolde dies at the end. The dissonant chromaticism that characterizes Tristan literally raised the curtain on a new type of harmonic thinking, to be realized in succeeding generations. Wagner, ever the practical man of the theater, saw the necessity in this work for a relaxation of some of his theories and so we have a love duet and some choral writing while the leitmotifs tend to blend together rather than making more individual dramatic gestures. The Ring is the composer's longest work and the one that embodies his ideas most completely, but Tristan has perhaps the greater historical significance because of its harmonic language.

As one German season followed another, Metropolitan stockholders became restive under the high-toned seriousness of their entertainment. Expenses were down because of the reasons cited above, but by the time Siegfried was staged Henderson noted that "There is no doubt that the brilliant array of society people . . . were extremely bored."[13] After all, they were more interested in each other than the performance. The opera was a place to go after dinner and see one's friends, as social leader Mrs. Caroline Astor did, always arriving at her box at nine no matter when the curtain rose, and receiving friends between the acts.[14]

While the German accents of the Metropolitan dominated the scene, other types of opera had not totally disappeared from New York. Of major importance were two enterprises we will discuss shortly: Mapleson's company and the American Opera Company. Of lesser importance were other traveling troupes that offered sporadic performances of Italian operas in the remainder of the decade of the 1880s. Notable among these was Adelina Patti's wildly successful first farewell series (at the Metropolitan) in the spring of 1887 and the return the following year of Italo Campanini, tenor turned impresario, to premiere Verdi's Otello, which got only a lukewarm reception. In the spring of 1890 Henry Abbey and Maurice Grau presented an Italian season that highlighted Patti with Arditi and some members from Mapleson's old company.

THE GRAND TOURS

After his initial successful battle, as he termed it, with the Metropolitan in its opening months, Mapleson undertook another extensive tour. While at the Academy the usual brief trips to Brooklyn had been made, with longer ones to Philadelphia and Boston and even a trek to Montreal for four nights followed by a return to New York in early January. Later that month he started a lengthier journey, pausing first in Philadelphia and Baltimore and then progressing on to Chicago. Abbey, on tour with the Metropolitan, managed to appear in Philadelphia and Chicago at the same time as Mapleson, but the ploy was self-defeating, as the latter won the greater acclaim. In Chicago the companies, by chance, even stayed at the same hotel as they played out the competition from which they seemed unable to withdraw no matter how devastating it became.[15] Although Mapleson had planned to go on to Cincinnati for the Opera Festival, of which he had been a vital part in the past, serious floods forced a change of route to Minneapolis for three performances and then on to the scheduled week in St. Louis, where Abbey had just preceded him. From there Mapleson's company wended its way through Kansas City, St. Joseph, Denver, Cheyenne, and Salt Lake City to San Francisco, where it stayed for three weeks in March. It then returned to New York for a further week and a half of opera.

Travel conditions had improved considerably since the late 1860s, when Kellogg complained of slow trains without sleeping or dining cars so that: "Sometimes we had to sit up all night and were not able to get anything to eat . . . . The journeys were so long and so difficult that they used to say Pauline Lucca always travelled in her night gown and a black velvet wrapper."[16]

Mapleson described his train as:

Plenty of room for everybody. The prima donnas had their different cars. We had three cooks constantly employed working for ourselves and Patti . . . [whose car was] . . . the most elegant affair imaginable; . . . The walls are covered with embossed leather, the painting by Parisian artists; it is in cloth of gold and cost 65,000 dollars.[17]

Elsewhere Mapleson noted the woodwork and Steinway piano of sandalwood and the solid silver used for the bath with its hot and cold water.

If travel had improved, keeping peace between prima donnas in the same company had not. Mapleson, however, proved himself an artist at tactful mediation. When Gerster saw Patti's name on a playbill in Baltimore in larger print than her own and discovered that tickets were higher priced for Patti's performances than hers, she flounced out of the tour and back to New York. So Mapleson had to change that evening's scheduled opera in which she starred and, because she had informed no one of her destination, track down the enraged singer in New York, whence he rushed by train to soothe the wounded ego. The feud continued in Chicago when Gerster received an ovation after Act I of Les Huguenots and Patti, whose part in that act was brief, was mistakenly presented with the many bouquets intended for a later act. Patti looked ridiculous, knew it, and swore she would never again sing in the same opera with Gerster. Later on, when Patti was kissed publicly and enthusiastically by the Governor of Missouri, and Gerster was asked if this was improper (these were Victorian times), she archly replied that there was no harm in a man kissing a woman old enough to be his mother. The intrigues, backbiting, and bickering were constant and required all of Mapleson's extraordinary diplomacy to manage and, whenever possible, to use for advantageous publicity.

He opened his three-week San Francisco season on March 10, 1884, with Gerster in Lucia, followed two nights later by the same star in L'elisir d'amore and then Patti's appearance in La traviata. Other operas performed included Rigoletto, La sonnambula, I puritani, Il trovatore, Martha, La favorita, Faust,

Crispino e la comare (Crispino and the Fairy) and Linda di Chamounix. The Grand Opera House had been refurbished and, according to Mapleson, "in the centre facing the main door was a huge crystal fountain, having ten smaller jets throwing streams of eau de Cologne into glass basins hung with crystal pendants. All over the vestibule were the rarest tree orchids, violets in blossom and roses in full bloom."[18] Publicity events surrounding the performances included an evening orchestral serenade at Patti's hotel (the Palace) and a ball given for her that the Italian and Russian consuls attended. Patti herself had a tremendous publicity build-up and was wildly acclaimed. Ticket scalpers and forgers had a field day that later resulted in the arrest of four men. Even Mapleson was arrested for violation of the theater's fire code and this startling, if unwarranted event, added extra color to the scene. As a final touch of drama a minor earthquake, which Patti attributed to Gerster putting the "evil eye" on the company, took place the day before the company left.

Despite the success of the extended tour, Mapleson had accumulated considerable debt. His contract with the stockholders at the Academy ran for another year, but they initially refused to pick up the bills from the tour and in fact, perhaps irritated by the manager's continuing financial demands, had Mapleson's props, scenery and costumes removed from the Academy, intending to put them up for sale. All was smoothed over eventually, however, and Mapleson returned after his usual summer of opera in London for two more seasons under the Academy's auspices.

These last seasons and tours followed the route and repertory of the one already outlined, with some modifications. The striking success of the first would reemerge in the second, but the last ended in disaster. Since the friction between Gerster and Patti had become too distracting and disruptive, Mapleson engaged, as Gerster's replacement, a young American named Emma Nevada, who had sung under him in London at Covent Garden. Although Nevada brought the luster of being a native daughter, she lacked Gerster's stunning skill and experience. Also new songs were sounding as the Metropolitan Opera, which had modestly toured only three cities that spring, was eliciting strong support and approval for its German repertory and new singers. Mapleson was unconcerned, however, for he planned to capitalize on the twenty-fifth anniversary of Patti's debut combined with her farewell visit. This was the first of her many farewell performances that stretched over almost thirty years to 1914.

One of Patti's strongest roles, which she sang in many cities across the country, was Aida. Verdi's lavish masterpiece, which appeared in New York less than two years after the world premiere in Cairo, held strong appeal for the "Gilded Age." Written for a commission by the Egyptian government to celebrate the opening of the Suez Canal, the composer created a "grand opera" for this great event, setting it, appropriately, in Egypt's colorful ancient past. The juxtaposition of personal feelings with national loyalty forms the crux of a plot surrounded with elaborate pomp and spectacle. The grandiose ending of Act II (the "Triumphal Scene"), which calls for choruses of priests, slave-prisoners and crowds, dancers, a brass band, and the soloists, is then followed by the opening of Act III (the "Nile Scene"), set at night on the shores of the Nile with a half hidden temple of Isis and an off-stage chorus. The one is all massed groups of people praising hero and country with brilliant, massive sound, while the other is set on a shadowy stage with quiet, delicately colored music as Aida sings of memories of the past and of her homeland. In sum, Aida focuses on intense feelings, rivalries and jealousies of the main characters in a setting that, like the pyramids, is larger than life.

While Verdi still used set numbers of aria, duet, chorus, and recitative, there is a greater fusion of sections so that musically this was a break from the past for him. In contrast to Wagner, however, one can still easily separate out individual pieces and, although the orchestra has assumed richer colors than in the past, it still functions mainly as accompanist and to provide background atmosphere. Imaginative instrumentation paints the Egyptian scenes with a greater complexity and subtlety of harmonic language than previous works such as Il trovatore. Aida, with all its excessive theatrical tinsel, was a brilliant success everywhere.

In his last American tour, Mapleson's company lacked the powerful Patti but included Minnie Hauk, Lillian Nordica, Luigi Ravelli, and Giuseppe Del Puente. New works were Wallace's Maritana and Massenet's Manon, accompanied by a repeat of the previous year's revival of L'Africaine. The New York season was "disastrous" (Mapleson's word) financially, and as the tour progressed, illness struck repeatedly (even the tireless and indispensable Arditi), box office receipts were down, and more feuds boiled up between singers. A dramatic one erupted between Hauk and Ravelli during a performance of Carmen, when Hauk violently and unexpectedly embraced her Don José as he was about to utter a spectacular high note that became a squawk. At the end of the act, Ravelli rushed about backstage, threatening to kill the soprano, terrorized the other singers, and continued to be so threatening that he was eventually withdrawn from the role. By the end of two weeks in San Francisco, chorus and orchestra had been ousted from their hotels because of lack of payments, and Ravelli was suing Mapleson for back wages. In the disastrous trip back across the country the frantic Mapleson, who was also acting as chef and butler for his disconsolate company, periodically had to sell costumes and scenery to pay for the rail fares, confront a brief strike of the chorus by cutting all the choral parts in Lucia and handle a strike by the orchestra.[19] He returned to England to produce opera for a few years, but his American career was over.

OPERA IN ENGLISH ENCORE

During the second half of the 1880s the American Opera Company had been formed and began touring with almost as much publicity as Mapleson's, if with vastly different aims. The central ideas were to present opera in English with American singers, encourage American composers and librettists and start a school that would train future singers free of charge. In the near future similar companies and schools, inspired by the tours of the original one, were envisioned as springing up in major cities across the country. The person who conceived this ambitious and innovative plan was a highly intelligent, Paris Conservatory trained, wealthy woman named Jeannette Thurber, who helped finance an impressive number of musical enterprises over the next few decades.[20] As the musical director for the American Opera Company, she hired Theodore Thomas, whose concerts for young people she had supported earlier and who was well known throughout the country for his orchestra tours. Thomas's orchestra would be used, and the approach, which the conductor strongly supported, would be ensemble rather than star oriented. Theodore Thomas, hitherto connected with instrumental music, now brought his considerable fame and zeal to opera. A first-class musician, this rather stiff-necked Victorian, besides his accomplishments noted earlier, had been a founder of the Cincinnati May Festival, had directed the Philadelphia Centennial concerts of 1876 and would, in 1891, become first conductor of the new Chicago Symphony. Up to now his dealings had been primarily with players in an orchestra, where he himself had started out. He had limited operatic experience and little sympathy for the singer's problems or point of view and less for the fluctuating temper of a prima donna. Typically, on a tour to San Francisco in 1883 with his orchestra, he had rigidly refused to allow soprano soloist Emma Thursby to give the customary encores, much to the annoyance of singer and audience. Apparently he thought it would interfere with the program's continuity and deflect attention from music to performer. That was the Thomas style.

The American Opera Company opened on January 4, 1886, with German composer Hermann Goetz's The Taming of the Shrew, which had been translated into English and performed by the Carl Rosa Company in London. Other works included Gluck's Orpheus and Euridice, Lohengrin, The Magic Flute, The Merry Wives of Windsor, Lakmé (an American premiere), The Flying Dutchman and Victor Massé's The Marriage of Jeannette on a double bill with Delibes' ballet, Sylvia.[21]

The company then toured with enthusiastic receptions in Boston and Washington, but somewhat less acclaim in Philadelphia and Baltimore. Problems arose in St. Louis, where a well-known social leader protested the suggestiveness (in her eyes) of the ballet costumes, and again in Chicago as Thomas and soprano Helene Hastreiter argued over the latter's billing compared to Emma Juch's. Unlike Mapleson, Thomas was impatient rather than conciliatory with soloists and unable, because of his reserved personality and seriousness of style, to milk such events for their possible publicity. In the opera company's favor was the strong reputation and following Thomas had already created through his many tours with his orchestra. Despite some financial pressures incurred by lavish spending on costumes and sets and frequent criticism of the leading soloists, the company ended the year successfully with commitments to start up schools, following Mrs. Thurber's model, from most of the cities toured.

The American Opera Company's second season opened in Philadelphia in November 1886 with Faust and a better response from the public, but some severe words from critic Krehbiel regarding the leading tenor. Aida and Les Huguenots joined the repertory and French soprano Emmy Fursch-Madi the company. She and Thomas shortly became locked in battle in St. Louis over the staging of Les Huguenots, which she had sung under Meyerbeer himself in Paris and about which she held firm views. Then the corps de ballet again came under attack, this time by the combined forces of the Women's Christian Temperance Union and the Evangelical Alliance, for its "spectacular representations of sensuality [that] are manifestly immoral in their influence."[22] To compound the situation, in Chicago the dancers' costumes, which had been altered for the Lakmé production to avert criticism, were roundly panned as ridiculous.[23] Nevertheless, the company, which changed its name to the National Opera Company in 1887, weathered its storms, as lawsuits and problems between Thurber and Thomas were somewhat resolved, and consolidated its reputation on the tour.

Financial problems, however, remained, worsening with the company's production of Nero by Anton Rubinstein and a tour to San Francisco. Nero's scenic design and costumes, mounted in lavish fashion, attracted more praise than the composer's lengthy, if undistinguished, music. Thomas's choice of the work and his refusal to make cuts reveal his further limitations as an opera conductor. Faced with such a work, a Maretzek or a Mapleson would have taken the expedient path of shortening it. Expenses from the preceding season, losses from Nero and the more extensive tour to the West Coast sadly enough ended in financial disaster and the company's demise. Mrs. Thurber had generously supported her high goals, but Thomas's inexperience with opera and its workings as a totality led to some mediocre choices of works and strains with singers. Less obvious, but equally important, was that it takes more than a few performances and a few years to forge the direction of an art form.

Mrs. Thurber had, however, also considered the long-term aspect, for, if her opera companies were financial failures, her National Conservatory of Music was a landmark institution for a quarter of a century after its opening in 1885. The notion of a national conservatory had been mentioned earlier in journals such as Harper's, and in 1872 a National College of Music had been founded in Boston. A disastrous city-wide fire in the first year of the College hampered enrollment, caused students to withdraw and thus undermined the financial stability of the institution, which failed in its second year. The initial purpose of Thurber's school, modeled on the Paris Conservatory which she had attended, was to train singers for the American Opera Company. By the late 1880s it had enticed such internationally recognized musicians as pianist Rafael Joseffy, soprano Ilma di Murska, and conductor Anton Seidl to its staff, plus the impressive addition of Antonin Dvorak as director.[24] An article appeared in The Forum (1892) less than a year before Seidl's appointment to the staff, in which he eloquently called for opera translated into English and the training of American singers. The following year in the same journal, composer Silas Pratt assessed Jeannette Thurber's effort with suggestions for the future.

After the collapse of the National Opera Company, one of its singers, Emma Juch (1860-1939) formed her own company to continue performances of opera in English. She had grown up in New York, but made her debut under Mapleson in London as Filina in Mignon in 1881 and sang with his company for the next three seasons, part of them on his American tours. She then joined Theodore Thomas for his tour of 1884, which combined orchestral works with unstaged excerpts from Wagner's music dramas. Amalie Materna, later at the Metropolitan and Herman Winkelmann, Wagner's choice for the first Parsifal, were also soloists with Juch. With a well established reputation, she now went on to sing in Jeannette Thurber's company and then to form the Emma Juch Grand English Opera Company in 1889 with Thurber's former manager, Charles Locke. Their company performed in New York at Oscar Hammerstein's Harlem Opera House to mixed notices that praised Juch's artistry but found the rest of the cast well below her caliber and criticized awkward staging.[25] The translated repertory brought Mignon, Carmen, Der Freischütz, Faust, The Bohemian Girl, The Postilion of Lonjumeau (A. Adam), Rigoletto, Il trovatore, Lohengrin, La Gioconda, The Trumpeter of Säckingen (V. Nessler), and other works to many cities from Boston to Cleveland, to St. Louis, to the Houston-Galveston area, and beyond. Touring lasted for two seasons.

FESTIVALS AND OTHER CITIES

Cincinnati had moved toward major musical and cultural prominence when Theodore Thomas founded the May Festival in 1873. A new concert hall was completed to open the third May Festival five years later, and then in the early 1880s an opera festival was initiated under the guidance of Max Maretzek with Mapleson's company. The large-scale planning of high-quality performances won Cincinnati an eminent place in the country operatically. Besides the orchestra of 150, Mapleson had organized a chorus of 350 local singers to supplement his own chorus of 400 for the opening of Lohengrin. There followed The Magic Flute with Gerster as the Queen of the Night, Boito's Mefistofele, Lucia coupled with one act of Rossini's Moses in Egypt, then Aida, La sonnambula, and finally Faust. For this highly successful festival Mapleson received $34,000, Patti $14,000, and the Festival realized $16,000.[26] The following year (1882) the festival, again with Mapleson, opened with Meyerbeer's Les Huguenots (still the orchestra of 150 but now only 400 in the chorus!), followed by Faust (a substitution for Il trovatore, which Patti had to cancel because of a cold), Carmen, Fidelio, William Tell and Lohengrin. The same year Mapleson revived L'Africaine, which he describes as:

> fine spectacle. . . The great ship scene of the third act created a perfect furor. . . . The grand march too in the fourth act created a sensation, equally with the magnificent spectacle and the gorgeous palanquin in

which Selika enters. . . . I had requested [the design of] a full sized elephant with a palanquin on its back, in which people were seated, the interior of the elephant being occupied and kept firm by two stalwart policemen.[27]

Mapleson's participation in the Cincinnati Festival of the spring of 1883 was, if anything, according to him, more successful than the previous ones. The repertory added The Flying Dutchman and Don Giovanni but otherwise remained the same. It is worth noting that, except for Mephistofele, Carmen, and The Flying Dutchman, the rest of the repertory dated from the 1850s and before. The Courthouse Riots cast a pall over the fourth Opera Festival, but equally important, the "great" flood hampered all transportation in and out of the city. A fifth Opera Festival was undertaken, under new administrative management, that brought in the American Opera Company with Thomas on its second tour. Despite Thomas's addition to his repertory of some conservative, well-known works (Les Huguenots, Faust, and Aida), support of talented singers such as Emma Juch and Jessie Bartlett Davis and initial enthusiasm by press and public, profits were meager. By now, Cincinnati's eminent position in the Midwest was on the wane.

In addition to its opera festivals, the city welcomed and praised the youthful Walter Damrosch, who brought the German repertory of the Metropolitan to Cincinnati in 1885. The following year Mapleson included Cincinnati on his disastrous "retreat," as he called it, from San Francisco. A variety of French, Italian and English traveling companies performed in Cincinnati over the next fifteen years, from Minnie Hauk's few such ventures to Emma Abbott's many. One especially praised was Damrosch's German Company with Max Alvary, Johanna Gadski and Emil Fischer. When the Metropolitan began including Cincinnati in its tours of the late 1890s with such stars as Emma Calvé, Jean and Edouard de Reszke and Ernestine Schumann-Heink, a more predictable continuity developed.

As Cincinnati waned, Chicago waxed in importance, with Mapleson's two weeks of performances in 1885 billed as the "First Chicago Opera Festival." The first performance of The Ring cycle would follow at the end of the decade. By the early part of the

1890s the confluence of railroads from the East, West, and South made Chicago the transportation hub of the Midwest. The founding of the University of Chicago and the arrival of Theodore Thomas as first conductor of the Chicago Symphony added considerably to the city's cultural stature. The Auditorium, built by architect Louis Sullivan, opened with Patti in Gounod's Roméo et Juliette. Her managers, Abbey and Grau, also had Verdi's Otello in the repertory, with Francesco Tamagno, who had created the title role under the composer's direction. Soon Damrosch and Lehmann brought their strong conceptions of German opera to the Auditorium and shortly thereafter Abbey and Grau returned with French and Italian opera sung by Emma Eames, Lehmann, her husband, tenor Paul Kalisch and the de Reszke brothers. The tour ended with a presentation of the fourth acts of Trovatore and Otello respectively, Act II of Barber of Seville and Act III of Carmen, a typical mélange of the time loved by audiences and fostered by managers.[28] Two years after the Columbian Exposition of 1893, momentum increased as the Metropolitan brought Carmen with Emma Calvé, described by Henderson as "a creature of unbridled passion, with a sensuous, suggestive grace . . . careless of all consequences."[29] The Metropolitan kept its conservative position firm on its tours to Chicago with Melba in Lucia and an all-star Huguenots but nodded to the contemporary with Tamagno in Otello, while Damrosch produced a consistent Wagner series with Johanna Gadski and the famous Alvary and Fischer. For the remainder of the decade, the Metropolitan gave conventional, well-known works with the exceptions of Mascagni's Cavalleria rusticana (Rustic Chivalry) and Massenet's La Navarraise (The Girl from Navarre), and Damrosch staged French and Italian as well as German works. Henry Savage's Castle Square Opera successfully offered light opera and English translations of familiar works done mainly by American singers at Studebaker Hall.[30] The French Opera Company from New Orleans brought greater variety when it arrived with a repertory including Halévy's La Juive and Gounod's La Reine de Saba (The Queen of Sheba).

Opera in New Orleans after the Civil War was performed mainly at the French Opera House, an example of American Greek Revival architecture designed by James Gallier. This burned in

1919, with all of its scores, librettos, books and records, so to have a better picture of singers, works and general history, fairly extensive research still needs to be done. A number of impresarios leased the French Opera house over the years for performances and a substantial number, seventeen, of American premieres were performed there from 1886 to 1912. An impressive group of composers, including, Massenet, Saint-Saëns, Godard, Giordano and Cilèa wrote those works, among which the best known are Saint-Saëns' Samson et Dalila (1893), Massenet's Manon (1894) and Cilèa's Adriana Lecouvreur (1907).[31] Because the premieres were all by French composers it seems likely that strong links were maintained to Paris by managers and troupes.

EAST COAST IN THE 1890s

As the "Gilded Age" entered the final decade of the century, the Metropolitan's repertory briefly shifted from Wagner back to Italian and French works; concurrently, a new point of view developed regarding the singing of opera in its original language; and the star again became the focus of productions rather than the ensemble. And many extraordinary stars there were in this so-called "Golden Age" of opera. Singers who were most popular with the public were retained in the company, thus providing consistency and stability. As ideas about language changed, possibilities for planning a wider repertory developed. German opera, meantime, remained on other New York stages, in large part because of the efforts of Walter Damrosch and reappeared at the Metropolitan in about the middle of the decade. Finally, Cavalleria rusticana in 1891, Pagliacci in 1893 and Tosca in 1901 ushered in the new style of verismo.

Reasons for the turn to an Italian and French repertory were financial rather than aesthetic. Despite the music dramas' profitable aspect, interest in Wagner by the stockholders at the Opera House had diminished, their restlessness and gossiping during performances rising with their boredom. The ticket purchasers in the audience, who had a more attentive attitude, complained repeatedly about the frequently distracting conversation coming from the boxes. Henderson characterized the controversy in The Times with open sarcasm, and in January 1891 the Board of Directors issued a politely worded notice to box holders requesting silence. Besides the stockholder's boredom with Wagner, the remaining audience balked at the third-rate Germanic novelties, such as Alberto Franchetti's weak emulation of Wagner, Asrael, or the Duke of Saxe-Coburg's amateurish Diana von Solange about which Henderson gloomily reported that "There may be many reasons for the productions of Diana von Solange, but it would be difficult to discover them."[32] Ticket sales slumped, and clearly the limitations of a German-based repertory had to be rethought. The directors sought a solution by contracting with Henry Abbey for a season of Italian and French works.

The opening night of Gounod's Roméo et Juliette signaled new repertory and three major new singers: Emma Eames and Jean de Reszke in the title roles and Édouard de Reszke as Frère Laurent. Henderson reported enthusiastically that Jean de Reszke was "a man of genuine artistic feeling and of high vocal accomplishments." and his brother Édouard was "a really great artist. His voice magnificent in power and range."[33] The strong European reputations of the Polish de Reszke brothers plus the beautiful, youthful Eames, who had been coached in her role as Juliette by Gounod himself, lent considerable luster to Abbey's company. Soon Nordica, famous from her performances with Mapleson and at the Metropolitan, would join the company, as would the great French baritone from the Paris Opéra, Jean Lassalle.

The ability and willingness of the de Reszkes, Eames, and Nordica to learn and sing roles in the original language gave the impetus to start the custom that has generally prevailed ever since. Jean de Reszke initiated the idea under Seidl in November 1895 with his first Tristan in German, a language he took the trouble to learn and in which he became fluent. This approach did not happen overnight, and the Italian Meistersinger and Tannhäuser in the previous year may have disappointed the German section of the audience, although they probably welcomed Wagner's return in any form.

Over the century, the prevailing language in which opera

was sung had gone from English to Italian to German. When a certain language dominated, because of the manager and nationality of his troupe, other works were translated into it. Faust had been sung in Italian, then German, then English, depending on the company and singers or conductor. Finally, opera began to be sung in the language of the original libretto, signifying a recognition of the importance of the integrity of the work in comparison to the importance of the performer. This would lead to another challenge for the performer, for besides a greater language ability, a vocal style different from that of Italian opera was required by Wagnerian roles. In the works after Lohengrin, Wagner's "endless melody" and enlarged orchestra required greater volume and projection and a different type of phrasing. Also, one had to memorize differently, for there was little text repetition and the musical repetitions, again of a different type, tended to remain in the orchestra. Whereas in the past, few artists had needed or attempted to master differing languages or musical and acting styles of an Isolde, Rosina or Marguerite, now the prospect was more imminent.

The era of what de Reszke called "international opera" had begun. The French and Italian casts were stronger in the beginning, as slowly all works were returned to their original tongue. The polyglot performance, in which soloists or chorus each sang in a different language, would, however, reappear sporadically for a long time. Managers Abbey and Grau followed the Wagnerian lead of Jean de Reszke and reinstated some German works. Seidl, who had been consolidating his reputation by conducting instrumental groups in the absence of opera, was hired to conduct, and Damrosch's influence was also felt.

About the time of the Metropolitan's return to German opera (1894), Walter Damrosch hired famous Wagnerian singers Materna and Fischer to give two charity benefit performances of Die Walküre at Carnegie Hall; these were very well received. A newly formed Wagner Society, supported by Damrosch, plus a petition to the Metropolitan's Board supported by Seidl, brought pressure for more German works. The rivalry between Seidl and Damrosch to conduct the proposed repertory, however, became an obstacle that precluded any change. Damrosch lost that battle, but, undaunted, formed a company of German singers hired in Europe and as manager and conductor staged sixteen subscription performances of Wagner that were successful financially. He then toured Boston, Cleveland, St. Louis and, as noted, Cincinnati and Chicago, receiving acclaim everywhere. For the next three years Damrosch continued to head his German company with reasonable success in the East and West but not in New Orleans with its strong allegiance to French opera.[34] By the time he took on Charles Ellis as manager, however, he too had expanded to operas in French and Italian as well as German.

Maurice Grau's partner Henry Abbey, died in 1896, as did the strong Metropolitan supporter, William Steinway, who had aided in the company's financial reorganization earlier. Two years later the company suffered another major loss when Anton Seidl died. As the century closed, Grau's policy was to keep the best and most popular singers, many of whom we have already mentioned, and maintain the works in which those singers excelled. Operas most frequently performed in the 1898 and '99 seasons were: Faust, Lohengrin, Carmen, Tannhäuser, Roméo et Juliette, and Die Walküre. Those receiving only one performance were: Martha, Mignon, Die Lustigen Weiber von Windsor (The Merry Wives of Windsor), Fidelio and Pagliacci.[35]

This last work, along with its companion, Mascagni's Cavalleria rusticana, represented the style of opera known as verismo, whose primary importance lay in Italy and which lasted about two decades. The subjects, which emphasized an unvarnished realism and violence in contemporary settings, had roots in the French literary "naturalism" of Zola and Maupassant but as solitary melodramatic segments without the development of character or plot found in the French authors' works. Intensity of orchestral harmony and color heighten the tension, and the vocal line adopts a declamatory style that shows traces of late Verdi. To a great degree, arias, recitatives, and other set pieces had been abandoned. Another example of verismo is Puccini's Tosca of 1900, based on a play made famous by Sarah Bernhardt.

Grau continued as manager at the Metropolitan until failing health in 1903 forced his retirement. His tenure had been marked by his ability to bring large numbers of first-class singers to New

York, his cool business approach that closed the company in 1898 for financial reasons and the lengthy tour to the West Coast in 1900-1901. Grau introduced few new works, for he believed that it was the star that drew an audience, not the work, which would be initially expensive and might not create a following. While Tosca would become a staple work, other new operas he chose, such as famous pianist Paderewski's Manru and female composer Ethel Smythe's Der Wald (The Forest), proved unsuccessful.

PHILADELPHIA AND BOSTON

While Philadelphia and Boston shared much of the overflow of activity from New York, such as the periodic tours of the Metropolitan's company and those of Damrosch, they also maintained some individual operatic features. In Philadelphia Gustav Hinrichs, who had been an associate conductor with Theodore Thomas in the ill-fated National Opera Company, directed opera at the Grand Opera House from 1888, even adding a series of summer seasons. As important was his staging in the first half of the 1890s of American premieres of Mascagni's Cavalleria rusticana and L'amico Fritz (Friend Fritz), Bizet's The Pearl Fishers and Puccini's Manon Lescaut, all of which soon went on to New York. Damrosch became director of Philadelphia's Academy of Music in 1896, bringing his German works, and returned in the following year with greater variety of repertory.

In 1891 Boston had the benefit of Minnie Hauk's company with Del Puente and Galassi performing French and Italian works under the management of Charles Hess. Hinrichs' Grand Opera company also came with Italian opera. Henry W. Savage's large company offered popular prices in 1898 for a season of opera in English that consisted of Il trovatore, Carmen, Cavalleria rusticana, Pagliacci, and four operettas. Savage took the company to New York's Metropolitan a few years later, but with less success. His Castle Square Company, which originated in Boston, traveled for a number of years offering English translations of standard European fare along with productions of Gilbert and Sullivan's Pinafore and Mikado.

One of Boston's more unusual performances was the premiere of Walter Damrosch's first opera, The Scarlet Letter, which had a libretto by Hawthorne's son-in-law based on the novel. Boston was an appropriate place for this premiere with a cast that included the most famous American baritone of the day, David Bispham, the rising German star Johanna Gadski and well-known bass Conrad Behrens. The opera was repeated in New York but failed to enter any repertory perhaps either because of the libretto, which Krehbiel described as "undramatic in the extreme," or the music so reminiscent of its Wagnerian model.

CONCLUSION

The introduction of Wagnerian music dramas on a regular basis, with the accompanying shift to an ensemble orientation in performance style, and the demanding standards of Seidl and Lehmann left the strongest impressions on opera of the time. Although the star's prominence only briefly dimmed and would shortly be increased by Enrico Caruso's appearance, the case for strong ensemble had been made and would be remembered. Grau remained uninterested in conductors, but Seidl's compelling interpretive style impressed audiences, opening a new view of that role.[36] An Arditi, despite his fine qualities, did not have that type of emotional appeal. When singers, such as Nordica, Eames and de Reszke, initiated the idea of performing opera in its original language, it was a change that would have far-reaching implications for singers. Perhaps the most important event of the time was the establishment of a permanent home for opera at the Metropolitan. Whatever the problems, the benefits of financial stability and a consistent place in which to perform outweighed them.

Mrs. Thurber's hope of establishing opera companies across the land with singers trained in America was in part a response to the popularity of opera and seemed an idea whose time had come. She thought out her plan, funded it generously, hired committed, well-trained musicians but unfortunately lacked any experience in dealing with the possible problems of such an enterprise. Moreover, her first in command, Theodore Thomas, lacked the flexibility to change direction when necessary. Misguided choices, such as Rubinstein's Nero, tended to waste energy and money, while Thomas's rather rigid views and tactless attitude could lead to stand-offs with singers, such as the one with soprano Helene Hastreiter, whose contract was not renewed despite her excellence. Although Mrs. Thurber had stated that the American Opera Company would encourage American composers and librettists, no opera by an American was introduced.

NOTES

1. Sean Dennis Cashman, America in the Gilded Age: From the Death of Lincoln to the Rise of Theodore Roosevelt, 2nd ed. (New York: New York University Press, 1988), p. 194.
2. Harold Rosenthal, ed., The Mapleson Memoirs: The Career of an Operatic Impresario 1858-1888 (New York: Appleton-Century, 1966), p. 209.
3. John Cone, First Rival of the Metropolitan Opera (New York: Columbia University Press, 1983), pp. 9-10.
4. Ibid., p. 30.
5. Henry Edward Krehbiel, Chapters of Opera, 3rd rev. ed. (New York: Henry Holt and Company, 1911), p. 102.
6. Ibid., p. 87.
7. Ibid., p. 91.
8. Ibid., p. 175.
9. George Martin, The Damrosch Dynasty: America's First Family of Music (Boston: Houghton Mifflin Co., 1983). This excellent book provided some of the information concerning the Damrosch family.
10. Krehbiel, Chapters of Opera, pp. 130-131.
11. Lilli Lehmann, My Path Through Life Translated by Alice B. Seligman (New York: Arno Press, 1977), p. 367.
12. Krehbiel, Chapters of Opera, pp. 150-151.
13. Irving Kolodin, The Metropolitan Opera 1883-1966: A Candid History (New York: Alfred A. Knopf, 1968), p. 104.
14. Ibid., p. 66.
15. Mapleson, op. cit., p. 186.
16. Clara Louise Kellogg, Memoirs of an American Prima Donna (New York: G. P. Putnam's Sons, 1913), p. 28.

17. Mapleson, The Mapleson Memoirs, pp. 313-314.

18. Ibid., p. 197.

19. Ibid., Chapter 39.

20. Emanuel Rubin, "Jeannette Meyers Thurber and the National Conservatory of Music," American Music VIII/3 (1990), pp. 294-325.

21. Ezra Schabas, Theodore Thomas: American Conductor and Builder of Orchestras 1835-1905 (Chicago: University of Illinois Press, 1989). Much of the information on the American Opera Company and the National Opera Company came from this book.

22. Ibid., pp. 158-159.

23. Ibid., p. 160.

24. Rubin, "Jeannette Meyers Thurber." The article gives a comprehensive outline of the institution's life.

25. John Frederick Cone, Oscar Hammerstein's Manhattan Opera Company (Norman: University of Oklahoma Press, 1966), p. 9.

26. Schabas, Theodore Thomas, p. 113.

27. Mapleson, The Mapleson Memoirs, p. 153.

28. Edward C. Moore, Forty Years of Opera in Chicago (New York: Arno Press, reprint 1977), p. 28.

29. Kolodin, The Metropolitan Opera, p. 123.

30. Ronald Davis, A History of Opera in the American West (Englewood Cliffs, NJ: Prentice-Hall, 1965), p. 70.

31. Gwyn S. McPeek, "New Orleans as an Opera Center," Musical America LXXIV/4 (1958), p. 25.

32. New York Times, January 10, 1891.

33. Ibid., December 15, 1891.

34. Krehbiel, Chapters of Opera, p. 259.

35. Ibid., pp. 318-319.

36. Howard Shanet, Philharmonic: A History of New York's Orchestra (New York: Doubleday, 1975), p. 186.

Epilogue

The British-derived musical theater style in the North and French opéra-comique in the South characterized the early part of the century with a consistent flow of new works layered on older repertory. The Devil's Bridge of 1812 entertained in the North as did Richard Coeur-de-Lion, older by thirty years, in New Orleans, where contemporary opéra-comique became a cultural link to the homeland. Sentiments of strong patriotism, morality and the conviction that good must triumph over evil pervaded both operas, the various versions of Der Freischütz and were at the core of many works of the time. Reinagle's stable theater in Philadelphia began its decline as an important musical center with his death in 1809. By the 1820s New York had replaced Philadelphia in political, mercantile and musical affairs. Despite some superficial resemblances, the roots of English and French operas were quite different, namely, a strong spoken theater in England in which music was secondary and a long, uniquely French, operatic tradition, stretching back to mid-seventeenth century, in which music had a central place. Operatically we were two worlds: French New Orleans and English Philadelphia and New York.

If Garcia's introduction of Italian opera to New York in 1825 was a dramatic musical event, it was also a single event, for, despite efforts to establish consistent performances of Italian works, the first half of the century was a time in which English operas and operas in English were the norm. Garcia and Malibran briefly offered a new repertory and new standards for singers, but Charles

Horn created a wider impression and reputation as he sang in and promoted the most popular works of the day such as Der Freischütz, his own The Devil's Bridge, or Lacy's Cinderella. He was also well known through his many church, oratorio and concert appearances. Besides the Rossini and Mozart mixtures Henry Bishop whipped up, translated French and Italian operas became part of the repertory of English companies that traversed the theatrical circuits. Composer William Henry Fry introduced a highly successful English version of Norma starring the Seguins, which they then took on the road, playing in cities and towns from New York to New Orleans. Anne Seguin, whose fame was such that she became known as the "American Prima Donna," skillfully managed this solid company.[1] Translations of La sonnambula as well as Norma, with readily available sheet music, brought Bellini into the world of many amateur musicians who played and sang his works with varying degrees of expertise, but, apparently, with great enjoyment. The 1830s and 1840s were the heyday of the traveling English companies, the opera with a "happy ending" and a time when America expected shortly to produce fine musical works and when American composers still had hopes that their works would be performed.

In the next few decades those hopes faded as European works took over and became firmly entrenched. With the appearance of the Havana Opera Company, its Italian performances and Italian- trained singers, we see the beginnings of a long rivalry between English and foreign language opera. A manager like Maretzek was committed to first-class works of the repertory that he knew had been successful. Fortunately for him, groundwork had already been done by English companies singing their many translations. Maretzek understood, as did his colleagues, the importance of fine singers, "the star" and how to appeal to a wealthy audience. A famous foreign star had enough caché to raise the ticket prices while the aura of Old World culture would draw in the socially elite. The Civil War brought the curtain down on it all for a few years.

After the war, different types of companies proliferated and actually spread opera throughout a wider area. Opera in English was undertaken with fresh zeal, French and English operettas became popular, and more companies with Italian repertory, and a few with German, followed the railroads farther away from the East Coast. Women had a strong role in staging opera in English, as the Kellogg company illustrated. Clara Louise Kellogg, greatly admired for her vocal accomplishments by Richard Grant White, stepped past the restrictions of the Victorian era and her own rather prim and prudish attitudes to run a first-class troupe in a solid repertory. To her credit she had clear objectives that were not solely financial. With Gilbert and Sullivan we see a revival of English comic opera style that had been transformed by fine comic verse, contemporary subjects and well crafted, memorable melodies. Whatever limitations time has revealed in these operettas, the wonderful wit and dancing tunes that entertained so many remain to elicit smiles even today. Their humor and gaiety offered a bright color to the increasingly somber and serious quality of other opera. As repetition dulled the Italian repertory, managers sought to engage audiences through the new German style and older German works. By this time the German population had swelled, German trained musicians held more orchestral positions and played more German music, and, significantly, Germany was viewed as the place for musical training.

The traveling Italian company with its "star" reached its zenith with Mapleson's lengthy, lavishly-styled tours. His financial collapse occurred as the new Metropolitan, of economic necessity, tried out a fresh approach. The new style, emphasizing ensemble rather than star, not only worked, but ushered in an innovative period in opera as Wagner's contemporary works were meticulously staged during seven seasons that culminated with the ambitious undertaking of the complete Ring cycle twice in 1889. If German works attracted a seriously attentive audience and won acclaim from critics, who were by now of crucial importance, it finally bored the wealthy stockholders less interested in edification than entertainment. Audience division was clear, and a return to the star system followed as French and Italian operas returned. A triple management of Abbey, Schoeffel and Grau lasted until 1897 when Grau became sole administrator. Under his direction a remarkable number of fine singers appeared consistently, as the custom of singing opera in the original language slowly was instituted. Although Mrs. Thurber's ambitious plan for the dissemination and support of opera in English failed, her legacy of a National Conservatory, with its distinguished faculty and fine curriculum, was an outstanding one.[2]

Meantime, the American composer stood ignored on the sidelines. For the Philadelphia Centennial Exhibition of 1876, reputable Americans John Knowles Paine and Dudley Buck were commissioned for a hymn and cantata respectively, but it was Wagner who received the huge $5,000 sum for a brief, ordinary march. Although operas by Americans were staged locally, and usually briefly, one would not be performed at the Metropolitan until Frederick Converse's The Pipe of Desire of 1910. That is not to say that Americans were idle or unsuccessful in other or related genres, for in fact they were busy producing a huge amount of music of all types, but opera was firmly entrenched behind doors not open to them.

When we first welcomed this charming foreigner she spoke our language in a style liked by many. Soon, however, she lapsed into other more exotic tongues, put on more expensive, even lavish, clothes and seemed to wish only to associate with the wealthy and well-born. While she offered a model of the past with admirable standards of musical taste and style, she also isolated herself from the more immediate world. On one level her expense and exclusivity became a competitive symbol of superiority and, as a by-product, a means of denigrating what was American because it was American. On another, she offered a memory of homeland, culture and language. She has always been varied, adaptable, glamorous and fascinating.

NOTES

1. John Curtis, "One Hundred Years of Grand Opera in Philadelphia." Unpublished typescript at the Historical Society of Pennsylvania in Philadelphia, p. 248.

2. Emanuel Rubin, "Jeannette Meyers Thurber and the National Conservatory of Music." American Music VIII/3 (1990), pp. 300-301.

Selected Bibliography

This list includes the major books and articles used as sources for this history, but does not include some of the references cited in each chapter's endnotes. Those have full bibliographic details. Also, the list omits the general reference tools, such as biographical and musical dictionaries, that were consulted.

Albrecht, Otto E. "Opera in Philadelphia 1800-1830." Journal of the American Musicological Society 32 (1979): 499-515.

Alexander, J. Heywood. It Must Be Heard: A Survey of the Musical Life of Cleveland, 1836-1918. Cleveland: Western Reserve Historical Society, 1981.

Arditi, Luigi. My Reminiscences. New York: Dodd Mead, 1896.

Armstrong, W. G. Record of the Opera in Philadelphia. Philadelphia: Porter & Coates, 1884. Reprint AMS, 1976.

Baily, Leslie. Gilbert and Sullivan and Their World. London: Thames and Hudson, 1973.

Barrett, William A. Balfe: His Life and Works. London: 1882.

Bispham, David. A Quaker Singer's Recollections. New York: Macmillan, 1920.

Bode, Carl, ed. American Life in the 1840s. New York: New York University Press, 1967.

Bogner, Harold F. "Sir Walter Scott in New Orleans, 1818-1832." Louisians Historical Quarterly 21 (1938): 420-517.

Boorstin, Daniel J. The Americans: The National Experience. New York: Random House, 1965.

Brown, T. A. History of the American Stage. New York: 1870. Reprint, 1969.

_____. History of the New York Stage from the First Performance in 1732-1901. New York: 1903.

Buckley, Peter George. "To the Opera House: Culture and Society in New York City, 1820-1860." Ph.D. dissertation, State University of New York at Stony Brook, 1984.

Bushnell, Howard. Maria Malibran: A Biography of the Singer. University Park, PA: Pennsylvania State University Press, 1979.

Carson, William. G. B. St. Louis Goes to the Opera, 1837-1941. St. Louis, Missouri: Missouri Historical Society, 1946.

_____. Theatre on the Frontier. Chicago: 1932.

Cashman, Sean D. America in the Gilded Age: From the Death of Lincoln to the Rise of Theodore Roosevelt. 2nd ed. New York: New York University Press, 1988.

Charlton, David. Grétry and the Growth of Opéra-Comique. Cambridge: Cambridge University Press, 1986.

Charvat, William. The Origins of American Critical Thought, 1810-1835. New York: Russell & Russell, 1968.

Clapp, William W. A Record of the Boston Stage. Reprint. New York: Greenwood Press, 1969.

Cone, John Frederick. First Rival of the Metropolitan Opera. New York: Columbia University Press, 1983.

Corder, Frederick. "The Works of Sir Henry Bishop." Musical Quarterly 4 (1918): 78-97.

Curtis, John. "A Century of Grand Opera in Philadelphia." The Pennsylvania Magazine of History and Biography 44 (1920): 122-157.

_____. "One Hundred Years of Grand Opera in Philadelphia." Unpublished typescript at the Historical Society of Pennsylvania in Philadelphia.

Dorman, James H., Jr. Theatre in the Ante Bellum South 1815-1861. Chapel Hill: University of North Carolina Press, 1967.

Dunlap, William. Diary of William Dunlap. Edited by Dorothy C. Barck, 3 vols. New York: The New York Historical Society, 1930.

Durham, Weldon B., ed. American Theatre Companies 1749-1887. Westport, CT: Greenwood Press, 1986.

Eisler, Paul E. The Metropolitan Opera: The First Twenty-Five Years, 1883-1908. Croton-on-Hudson, NY: North River Press, 1984.

Estavan, Lawrence, ed. San Francisco Theater Research. History of Opera in San Francisco. 8 vols. San Francisco 1939 WPA Project. Reprint, New York: AMS Press, 1972.

Farkas, Andrew. Opera and Concert Singers: An Annotated International Bibliography of Books and Pamphlets. New York: Garland Press, 1985.

Fiske, Roger. English Theatre Music in the Eighteenth Century. London: Oxford University Press, 1973.

Fitzlyon, April. Maria Malibran: Diva of the Romantic Age. London: Souvenir Press (E&A) Ltd., 1987.

Furnas, J. C. The Americans: A Social History of the United States, 1587-1914. Toronto: Longmans, 1969.

Gerson, Robert Aaron. Music in Philadelphia. Philadelphia: Theodore Presser Co., 1940.

Grimsted, David. Melodrama Unveiled: American Theater and Culture, 1800-1850. Chicago: University of Chicago Press, 1968.

Hamm, Charles. Yesterdays: Popular Song in America. New York: W. W. Norton & Company, 1979.

Hatch, Christopher. "Music for America: A Critical Controversy of the 1850s." American Quarterly 14 (1962): 578-586.

Hauk, Minnie. Memories of a Singer. New York: Arno Press, reprint, 1977.

Hipsher, Edward Ellsworth. American Opera and Its Composers: A Complete History of Serious American Opera, with a Summary of the Lighter Forms Which Led Up to Its Birth. Philadelphia: Theodore Presser Co., 1927.

Hitchcock, H. Wiley. "An Early American Melodrama." Notes 12 (1955): 375-388.

Hodges, Sheila. Lorenzo Da Ponte: The Life and Times of Mozart's Librettist. London: Granada Publishing, 1985.

Hoole, W. Stanley. The Ante-Bellum Charleston Theatre. Tuscaloosa: University of Alabama Press, 1946.

Ireland, Joseph N. Records of the New York Stage from 1750 to 1860. 2 vols. New York: Benjamin Bloom, 1966.

Jackson, Richard. Democratic Souvenirs: An Historical Anthology of Nineteenth-Century American Music. New York: C.F. Peters Corp., 1988.

Johnson, Claudia D. "That Guilty Third Tier: Prostitution in Nineteenth Century Theaters." American Quarterly 27 (1975): 575-584.

Johnson, H. Earle. "The Germania Musical Society." Musical Quarterly XXXIX/1 (1953): 75-93.

_____. Musical Interludes in Boston 1795-1830. New York: Columbia University Press, 1943.

Kaufman, Thomas G. "The Arditi Tour: The Midwest Gets Its First Real Taste of Italian Opera." Opera Quarterly 3 (1987): 39-52.

Kellogg, Clara Louise. Memoirs of an American Prima Donna. New York: G. P. Putnam's Sons, The Knickerbocker Press, 1913.

Kendall, John Smith. The Golden Age of the New Orleans Theater. Baton Rouge: Louisiana State University Press, 1952.

Klein, Hermann. The Reign of Patti. New York: The Century Co., 1920.

Kmen, Henry Arnold. Music in New Orleans: The Formative Years 1791-1841. Baton Rouge: Louisiana State University Press, 1966.

Kolodin, Irving. The Metropolitan Opera 1883-1966. A Candid History. New York: Alfred A. Knopf, 1968.

Krauss, Anne McClenny. "Alexander Reinagle, His Family Background and Early Professional Career." American Music 4 (1986): 425-456.

Krehbiel, Henry Edward. Chapters of Opera. 3rd rev. ed. New York: Henry Holt and Company, 1911.

Lafargue, Andre. "Opera in New Orleans in Days of Yore." Louisiana Historical Quarterly 29 (1946): 660-678.

Lawrence, Vera Brodsky. Strong on Music: The New York Music Scene in the Days of George Templeton Strong, 1836-1875. Vol. I, Resonances 1836-1850. New York: Oxford University Press, 1988.

_____. "William Henry Fry's Messianic Yearnings: Eleven Lectures, 1852-1853." American Music 7 (1989): 382-411.

Lehmann, Lilli. My Path Through Life. Translated by Alice Seligman. New York: G. Putnam and Sons, 1914.

McConachie, Bruce A. "New York Opera going 1825-50: Creating an Elite Social Ritual." American Music 6 (1988): 181-192.

McKay, David. "Opera in Colonial Boston." American Music 3 (1985): 133-142.

McKnight, Mark. "Wagner and the New York Press, 1855-76." American Music 5 (1987): 145-55.

Mapleson, J. H. The Mapleson Memoirs: The Career of an Operatic Impresario 1858-1888. Edited by Harold Rosenthal. New York: Appleton-Century, 1966.

Maretzek, Max. Revelation of an Opera Manager in Nineteenth-Century America. Crotchets & Quavers, Sharps & Flats. New York: Dover, 1968.

Martin, George. The Damrosch Dynasty: America's First Family of Music. Boston: Houghton Mifflin Co., 1983.

Mattfeld, Julius. A Hundred Years of Grand Opera in New York 1825-1925. New York: The New York Public Library, 1927.

_____. Variety Music Cavalcade 1620-1969. A Chronology of Vocal and Instrumental Music Popular in the United States. New York: Prentice-Hall, 1962.

Montague, Richard Addison. "Charles Edward Horn: His Life and Works (1786-1849)," Ph.D. dissertation, Florida State University, 1959.

Mussulman, Joseph A. Music in the Cultured Generation: A Social History of Music in America, 1870-1900. Evanston, IL: Northwestern University Press, 1971.

Odell, George Clinton Densmore. Annals of the New York Stage. 9 vols. New York: Columbia University Press, 1927-1937.

Offenbach, Jacques. Orpheus in America: Offenbach's Diary of His Journey to the New World. Translated by Lander MacClintock. Boomington: Indiana University Press, 1957.

Pessen, Edward. Riches, Class, and Power before the Civil War. Lexington, MA: D. C. Heath and Co., 1973.

Porter, Susan. With An Air Debonair: Musical Theatre in America 1785-1815. Washington, D.C.: Smithsonian Institution Press, 1991.

Pratt, Silas G. "A Plan and a Plea for American Opera." The Forum 15 (1893): 88-92.

Preston, Katherine Keenan. "Travelling Opera Troupes in the United States, 1825-1860." Ph.D dissertation, City University of New York, 1989. 2 vols.

Root, Deane L. American Popular Stage Music 1860-1880. Ann Arbor, MI: UMI Research Press, 1981.

Rubin, Emanuel. "Jeannette Meyers Thurber and the National Conservatory of Music." American Music 8 (1990): 294-325.

Schabas, Ezra. Theodore Thomas: America's Conductor and Builder of Orchestras, 1835-1905. Chicago: University of Illinois Press, 1989.

Schleifer, Martha Furman, ed. American Opera and Music for the Stage, 18th and 19th Centuries. Vol. 5 in Three Centuries of American Music. Boston, MA: G. K. Hall & Co., 1990

Seidl, Anton. "The Development of Music in America." The Forum 14 (1892): 386-93.

Seilheimer, George Overcash. History of the American Theatre. 3 vols. Grosse Pointe, MI: Scholarly Press, republished, 1968.

Shanet, Howard. Philharmonic: A History of New York's Orchestra. New York: Doubleday, 1975.

Singleton, Esther. "History of the Opera in New York from 1750 to 1898." The Musical Courier (1898): 23.

Smither, Nelle. A History of the English Theatre at New Orleans 1806-1842. New York: Benjamin Blom, Inc., reissued 1967.

Sonneck, Oscar G. T. Early Opera in America. New York: G. Schirmer, Inc., 1915; reprinted 1963.

Stone, James H. "Mid-Nineteenth-Century American Beliefs in the Social Values of Music." Musical Quarterly 43 (1957): 38-49.

Stoutamire, Albert. Music of the Old South: Colony to Confederacy. Rutherford, NJ: Fairleigh Dickinson University Press, 1972.

Tompkins, Eugene. The History of the Boston Theatre, 1854-1901. Boston: Houghton Mifflin Co., 1908.

Upton, William Treat. William Henry Fry American Journalist and Composer-Critic. New York: Thomas Y. Crowell Company, 1954.

Virga, Patricia H. The American Opera to 1790. Ann Arbor, MI: UMI Research Press, 1982.

Wemyss, Francis C. Chronology of the American Stage, from 1752-1852. New York: William Taylor, 1852

White, Richard Grant. "Opera in New York." The Century 23 (1882): 686-703, 865-882; 24 (1883): 31-43, 193-210.

Wolz, Larry Robert. "Opera in Cincinnati: The Years Before The Zoo, 1801-1920." Ph. D. dissertation, University of Cincinnati, 1983.

Yellin, Victor Fell. "Rayner Taylor." American Music 1 (1983): 48-71.

_____. "Rayner Taylor's Music for The AEthiop: Part 1, Performance History." American Music 4 (1986): 249-267.

_____. "Rayner Taylor's Music for The AEthiop: Part 2, The Keyboard Score (The Ethiop) and Its Orchestral Restoration." American Music 5 (1987): 20-47.

Index

About the Author

JUNE C. OTTENBERG is Professor of Music History Emerita at the Esther Boyer College of Music at Temple University, where she taught for many years. Her work with music in America has focused on musicians and music that immigrated to America from such places as England, Scotland, and Moravia. She contributes to various journals, has a chapter in the forthcoming *Opera in the Golden West*, and regularly publishes reviews of recordings in *High/Performance Review*.